G000310733

Catalina
Over
Arctic Oceans

CATALINA OVER ARCTIC OCEANS

Anti-Submarine and Rescue Flying in World War 2

Wing Commander John French
OBE, DFC, AFC, AE

Edited by Anthony L. Dyer

Pen & Sword
AVIATION

First published in Great Britain in 2013 by
Pen & Sword Aviation
an imprint of
Pen & Sword Books Ltd
47 Church Street
Barnsley
South Yorkshire
S70 2AS

Copyright © Anthony L. Dyer 2012

ISBN 978 1 78159 053 9

The right of Anthony L. Dyer to be identified as Author of this Work has been asserted by him in accordance with the Copyright, Designs and Patents Act 1988.

A CIP catalogue record for this book is available from the British Library

All rights reserved. No part of this book may be reproduced or transmitted in any form or by any means, electronic or mechanical including photocopying, recording or by any information storage and retrieval system, without permission from the Publisher in writing.

Typeset in Palatino by
Phoenix Typesetting, Auldgirth, Dumfriesshire

Printed and bound in England by
MPG Books Group

Pen & Sword Books Ltd incorporates the Imprints of Pen & Sword Aviation, Pen & Sword Family History, Pen & Sword Maritime, Pen & Sword Military, Pen & Sword Discovery, Wharncliffe Local History, Wharncliffe True Crime, Wharncliffe Transport, Pen & Sword Select, Pen & Sword Military Classics, Leo Cooper, The Praetorian Press, Remember When, Seaforth Publishing and Frontline Publishing

For a complete list of Pen & Sword titles please contact
PEN & SWORD BOOKS LIMITED
47 Church Street, Barnsley, South Yorkshire, S70 2AS, England
E-mail: enquiries@pen-and-sword.co.uk
Website: www.pen-and-sword.co.uk

Contents

Introduction

It is now almost twenty-five years since my Grandfather died. To us, his grandsons, he was known as Bandad (when children, we could not say Granddad!) and he was taken from us at far too young an age – sixty-seven years old.

To me, he was my personal hero; an instructor teaching bomber pilots to fly, followed by operations on RAF Catalina flying boats. He was a quiet, modest man, a superb cook and a loving Grandfather. On the day he died, I was coming home from University and was met at the train station by my Dad. He never usually picked me up, usually it was Mum, and so I knew immediately something was wrong. Bandad suffered from a hole in his heart throughout his life. When the murmur was first found during a pre-war aircrew medical, the doctor simply asked if he ever got tired or puffed out, as he did not, nothing else was said. In the 1960s his medical condition was properly identified and he had to leave service flying, which was a terrible blow. The doctor suggested that he should not get too excited – as Bandad's life to that point had been full of excitement this did amuse him! In 1986, the condition caught up with him. Bandad is always in my thoughts and my memories and I feel his presence around.

Several years before he died, he had finished his memoirs, but they remained unpublished. I have always wanted to share his story and some of his extensive photograph collection with others. I have not changed his words, only edited them and added notes where an explanation may help the reader, or where details from his diary have been added.

I dedicate this book to Bandad, Beatrice (his first wife) and their lovely daughter Valerie (my Mum!) and Nana (his second wife).

I would like to thank the family for encouraging me and my friends for their support.

Like Bandad, I hope you enjoy his memoirs and learn about one of this country's unsung heroes – my hero!

Tony Dyer, July 2012.

Original Introduction

This is an account of some events of my life which may be of interest to others (*typically modest nature of my bandad!*). They cover mainly flying and Eastern Europe over the last fifty years or so. The reader should not expect anything extraordinary, anything deeply analytical, but I hope that as he or she goes along, it will be found that we have something to share and enjoy together.

A lot of the book is about my friends but by no means about all of them. There have been and are so many, men and women, young and old, different races, different colours, different creeds, different positions in life; some of them I did not even know their names. Others could not stand the sight of some of the others – which presents a problem that must tax God himself, who loves all his creatures and creation, regardless of what they might think of one another.

With many of these friends I have lost touch – some still and always very dear to me; others have or may have died; others are very much alive. It is to all of them that I dedicate this book with love, in the sure hope and belief that we shall all meet again. But if one out of the company is to be named to represent the rest, then it is Bill McGuinty.

John French, 1980

List of Plates

Glossary of Terms

A&AEE	Aeroplane and Armament Experimental Establishment
AE	Air Efficiency Medal
AFC	Air Force Cross
AFL	Air Force Liaison
AOC	Air Officer Commanding
APA	Accident Prevention Advisor
APD	Accident Prevention Directorate
ASI	Air Speed Indicator
ASV	Air-to-Surface Vessel
ATA	Air Transport Auxiliary
ATS	Advanced Training School
AW23	Armstrong Whitworth 23 (type of aircraft)
BABS	Blind Approach Beam System
BEA	British European Airways
BEM	British Empire Medal
CFI	Chief Flying Instructor
CFS	Central Flying School
CO	Commanding Officer
D/F	Direction Finding
DFC	Distinguished Flying Cross
DH110	De Havilland 110 (type of aircraft)
DSO	Distinguished Service Order

EEC	European Economic Commission
ENSA	Every Night Something Awful
ETA	Estimated Time of Arrival
FTS	Flying Training School
GCS	Ground Control System, approach.
HP42	Handley Page 42 (type of aircraft)
HQ	Head Quarters
ITS	Intermediate Training School
LNER	London and North-Eastern Railway
MAEE	Marine Aircraft Experimental Establishment
MAP	Ministry of Aircraft Production
MC	Military Cross
MG	Morris Garages (type of car)
MO	Medical Officer/Orderly
MT	Motor Transport
MTB	Motor Torpedo Boat
NAAFI	Navy Army Air Force Institute
NATO	North Atlantic Treaty Organization
NCO	Non Commissioned Officer
OBE	Order of the British Empire
OTU	Operational Training Unit
PBY	Patrol Bomber – the Y is the Consolidated designation
PC	Political Correctness (not around between AD to 1990s!)
PLE	Prudent Limit of Endurance
PR	Photo Reconnaisence
PRU	Photo Reconnaisance Unit
QFI	Qualified Flying Instructor
QMC	Queen Mary College (University of London)
RAAF	Royal Australian Air Force

RAeS	Royal Aeronautical Society
RAF	Royal Air Force
RAFO	Royal Air Force Officer
RAFVR	Royal Air Force Volunteer Reserve
RCAF	Royal Canadian Air Force
RFC	Royal Flying Corps
RN	Royal Navy
RNVR	Royal Navy Volunteer Reserve
R/T	Radio Telephone or Receiver/Transmitter
SASO	Senior Air Staff Officer
TAF	Tactical Air Force
TMPFFS	Trim, Mixture, Pitch, Fuel, Flaps and Sperry
TO2	Training Operations/Organization
UB	Polish non uniformed police
ULAS	University of London Air Squadron
UN	United Nations
USAF	United States Air Force
USSR	Union of Soviet Socialist Republics
VC	Victoria Cross
VCAS	Vice Chief of Air Staff
VIP	Very Important Person
VTOL	Vertical Take-Off and Landing
V1	Vengeance weapon, Nazi, doodlebug
V2	Vengeance weapon, Nazi, rocket
WAAF	Womens Auxiliary Air Force
WO	Warrant Officer
WRAF	Womens Royal Air Force
WW1	World War 1
WW2	World War 2

CHAPTER ONE

How it all started

The flying bug bit me early in my life. One of my earliest memories is being in the garden of our house at Tadworth in Surrey – at the age of about four – noticing an 'airliner' on its way to Paris from Croydon, which had opened in 1920. So I set to work to construct an aircraft which had a very long fuselage made from an old trellis, and a rather precarious meat skewer strutted wing made of two planks. The tail surfaces were rather similar. The whole lot was mounted on a convenient inverted metal bowl. At this time, possibly more fun was obtained from the cut-out models on postcards, including seaplanes. Later, after we had moved to Felixstowe in 1925, I was to convert an unsatisfactory pedal car into a more satisfactory aircraft. Felixstowe provided plenty of aviation inspiration, for not only was there the air station – The Marine Aircraft Experimental Establishment (MAEE), where all seaplanes were tested, but only nine miles away was Martlesham Heath. This was the Aeroplane & Armament Experimental Establishment (A&AEE) which performed the same function as MAEE for all land planes.

Odd bits of old seaplanes and flying boats were scattered in dumps around the town and one dump, right in the centre, had several old hulls in it. It was not long before I cut my knee on one of these and I still have the scar to this day! This would have been on a piece of a Southampton, or something earlier. Down at Felixstowe Ferry were other hulls, including that of the Fairey

Atlanta, which was to last as a houseboat until the 1950s/60s, when it was burnt out. The Southampton hull now exhibited in the RAF Museum originated from the ferry.

Felixstowe certainly provided plenty of interest and excitement; the Schneider Trophy – a famous trophy awarded over many years to the fastest seaplane – teams trained there and there was a continual stream of new flying boats and seaplanes; big ones such as the Iris, Perth, Sarafand, the Empire Boats, Sunderland and Mayo Composite Experiment; and medium size Southamptons, now metal; Scapa, Stranraer, London and various other seaplanes. Just before the war came the Lerwick and the original PBY which led to the Catalina. Events such as the Beardmore Inflexible flying over from Martlesham, the R100 airship looming out of the clouds one morning, and the Graf Zeppelin later on, made life one continual parade of aviation development. An exciting sight one morning was the Fitzmaurice Junkers flying low over the town back to Germany, after its first abortive attempt in 1928 to fly from Europe to America.

It was not until my cycling got under way that the real attraction of Martlesham began. One early visit was notable when I saw a panel fall off a Hawker Fury doing aerobatics. I marked where it had fallen, recovered it and brought it back to deliver it to the pilot, who had meanwhile landed. A little later I was fortunate enough to have a visit to the airfield and was shown around the experimental hangars – now replaced by a Tesco Superstore – by Wing Commander E. G. Hilton DFC, AFC, one of the test pilots, a road at Martlesham Heath is named after him. Unfortunately, he was to be killed in the King's Cup Air Race at Scarborough in 1938. Around this time the prototype Wellington (K4049) crashed at Little Bealings and I visited the scene soon afterwards, removing a small piece of oil pump. Out at sea off Felixstowe, an early Magister spun and crashed, with the wing joint straps being washed ashore sometime later. I used them to mend my boat. These pre-war days also involved the early developments in radar at Bawdsey and of ASV (air-to-surface vessel), with aerials on some of the flying boats in Felixstowe. There were also the wandering Ju-52 aircraft of Lufthansa, which seemed frequently, though unsurprisingly, to make landfall by Bawdsey. But perhaps one of the most significant foretaste of years far ahead was to see the Curtiss Condors of an all-freight air service making landfall over Felixstowe.

As soon as I acquired a small still 16mm, six exposure Coronet Midget camera, price five shillings (twenty-five new pence), which supplemented my 620 Box camera and a big Kodak 3A won in a raffle, I began to indulge in some clandestine photography. The Midget was a stepping stone to a Karat 35mm, which I modified to take a 'telephoto' lens, home made from an aged aunt's monocular! I had to be more careful with the Karat, but my choice of location on the approach path soon put the game on a good footing! The main prizes to catch in 1936-1939 were the Spitfire, Hurricane, Defiant, Blenheim, Beaufort and the Botha. At an earlier stage there were the Harrow, the AW23 – forerunner of the Whitley – and the original prototype, a development of the Avro 652 high speed mail carrier, which was to become the Anson.

While still at Charterhouse school in Surrey I also made visits to Farnborough, mainly using the box camera. On one occasion, I was found within the rather ill-defined boundary and led out by an Air Ministry Policeman. I was escorted out the Main Gate, which was near Cody's Tree, this tree was used by Cody to tie his early aircraft to (Cody was an entrepreneur who toured Britain and the USA with the Wild Bill Cody's Western Show. Cody was also an aviation pioneer who developed and built the first ever aircraft for the British armed forces. The original tree developed rot and has been replaced with a fibre glass replica now). We went past the Hawker Audaxes of No.4 Squadron and the School of Photography. I photographed these behind the policeman's back with the Midget! Brooklands was another attraction and one year the King's Cup Race passed over the Hog's Back and we had a fine view (the Hog's back is a raised part of the picturesque land-scape of the North Downs in Surrey).

A fellow Farnborough visitor (our school bounds allowed free movement within an area bounded by railway lines, but Farnborough was outside) was John Derry. Because of the school bounds difficulty, we made separate visits, but shared observations and went to Hendon Air Display one year. Our paths crossed fleetingly during the next few years, with John becoming, after a period as wireless operator in No.269 Squadron on Hudsons in Iceland, a pilot on Typhoons. After the war, he became the finest test pilot and demonstrator of all time, until his tragic death in the De Havilland DH110 – not far from one of our favourite observation points which we used at Farnborough in those school days.

At school we had the occasional visit by aircraft, which used to land on one of the further fields not used for football or cricket. From this, grew the fascination of seeing aeroplanes landing and taking off from fields, not prepared aerodromes, with the long grass laid flat by the slipstream of the take-off and then the silence and emptiness as the excitement died down.

While at Charterhouse I made my first flight. Taking advantage of a holiday granted for the Royal Wedding of 1934 (Prince George and Princess Marina – the Duke and Duchess of Kent), I set off to Croydon to visit a caged bird show as the alleged purpose. But with that visit made, I was soon on my way by bus to Croydon Airport. After spending some time on the roof observing aeroplanes, I went downstairs and made my way as nonchalantly as possible up to the counter of Surrey Flying Services and booked a five shilling flight. There was a walk down from the main building to the hangars on Purley Way where there was a two-seat Gypsy III Moth. Once strapped in we were soon airborne, those five minutes did it! For months I remembered and relived almost every second of that flight. On getting back I recounted the day's events to my housemaster. Subsequently, I realized that he had been put in a dilemma, for I should have been punished for this action , but to his credit, I heard no more.

At this time I began my acquaintance with the *Aeroplane* magazine and its remarkable Editor, C.G.Grey, who in spite of his position, replied himself to my enthusiastic letters, or, if they were appropriate, passed them to Thurston James, his Technical Editor. Over the years it was clear that C.G.G. kept careful records of correspondence and nearly ten years later, even though I had not written for a few years, he wrote, "You were the schoolboy who kept on asking awkward questions." Possibly a reference to a question about the performance of the prototype Spitfire which I had seen and timed on a high-level run over Martlesham!

I managed to make two other flights from school. One of these was in the company of Pat Strathy, a brilliant science and mathematics student from Canada. In his small study at school, he devised a method of charging our wireless accumulators that depended on the use of an enormous number of 100 watt bulbs to reduce the voltage, but gave an enormous increase to the housemaster's electric bill! The scheme came to a rather sudden end, but without any punishment for Pat. Unfortunately, Pat was killed in action in HMS *Ajax* during the war and his death was one of those wartime losses of friends which even now are hard to bear. Similarly the loss of our mutual friend Desmond Watson in the Middle East was a shock. I got to know him even better after leaving school, when we used to meet regularly for an evening out. He drove his MG with elan and skill – 60 mph down Whitehall! However, it often made me think, as we went out, that the Sutton Harness in the Avro Tutor could well be adopted for car use!

One of the most memorable short flights at Croydon was one with Bill Ledley of Olley Air Services, who apologized for the grey dusty appearance of the interior of the Leopard Moth G-ACLM. He recounted how on the day before, he had been chartered to scatter someone's ashes over the channel. "Unfortunately," he said, "the ashes blew back into the aircraft and left me and the interior with a coating of the deceased! I

managed to scoop most of the ashes into a paper bag and jettisoned that." He was indeed embarassed when he reported to the
relatives that the job had been done, with a serious grey
countenance!

In 1934, I asked Surrey Flying services for a quote to carry me
home at the end of the School Holidays:-

Croydon to Ipswich (Gipsy Moth)	£5 15 shillings
(with a return at end of school holiday)	£11
Charterhouse to Ipswich	£7 10 shillings
(with a return at end of holiday)	£14

If I had taken my brother with me it would, by Puss Moth, have
been 25 per cent more.

All of this was leading up to the matter of how to learn to fly. My
first idea was to take up gliding; this caused horror to the family.
I had seen a gliding club on the Wasserkuppe in Germany in 1935,
when I had been on a cycle tour with the redoubtable "Alf"
Tressler, a fine teacher at Charterhouse and a friend. We had gone
from Cologne to Sarajevo in Yugoslavia, via Czechoslovakia and
Austria. We also got into the middle of some German military
manoeuvres with numbers of light tanks in use. There was some,
but not a lot of, aircraft participation, although in my diary I noted
various airfields and aircraft movements.

Then I read how a member of the University of London Air
Squadron (ULAS), a Mr Quertier, had had occasion to bale out of
his Avro 504. As I was going to be at the London Hospital Medical
College in January 1937, here was the answer on how I could fly.
Before I had even left school, I had arranged and had an interview
and been accepted as a medical student member of ULAS.

One other important event before I left school was that I
attended Arthur Gouge's RAeS lecture on the design and
construction of the Empire Flying Boats. This, combined with a
personally arranged visit to Rochester (Shorts) to see the boats

being built, and the prototype Sunderland K4774 surrounded with hessian, made my interest in this class of aircraft grow even further.

I went up to the London Hospital, but there was a month wait before a flying vacancy turned up. Ground training started at ULAS Headquarters in Exhibition Road in the evenings and early in the spring a flying vacancy appeared. Meanwhile my medical course started and I was not doing too badly.

In 1937, I sold my first aircraft photograph to the *Aeroplane*, and in 1938 managed to visit the cockpit of the Ensign, and later that of the Albatross (Frobisher), both at Croydon.

Early in 1938, after nearly a year in the ULAS, I joined the RAFVR (Royal Air Force Volunteer Reserve). To achieve that, and particularly because ULAS flying medical members were suddenly discontinued, I had to change faculties. I took up work at Queen Mary College (QMC) down the Mile End road. Later that year came Munich, the Prime Minister's 'Peace in Our Time'. On returning to QMC after the vacation, the then principal, Major General Sir Frederick Maurice, who had been to Munich to see Hitler personally during the days just before the 'Peace in Our Time' agreement, as a representative of ex-servicemen's interest in peace, called all the men students to a meeting. He told us, that, in his view, we would all be well advised to join the Territorials, RAFVR or RNVR (Royal Navy Volunteer Reserve) – war in his view, could not be avoided. This, in the middle of the post-Munich euphoria, was salutary advice. From an atmosphere of student interest and a lot of futile argument over the Spanish Civil War, there was a sharp change and many, if not most, took Sir Frederick's advice. Among the fellow students at QMC was Edgar Allies, who joined ULAS and was later to turn up at RAF South Cerney and then go on to serve on Hudsons in No.269 Squadron in Iceland, and later in the war on Liberators.

I started to cycle at a quiet time of day to visit the dark rooms, which could be hired at the London Photographic Centre in

Shaftesbury Avenue. The return ride in the rush hour could be a bit electric; I once had to go twice around Trafalgar Square, with 25 mph on my speedometer, before I could break out into Whitehall. Here, I learnt a lot about the techniques of enlarging and printing, which has stood me in good stead over the years. But, with my own equipment, I was to print pictures throughout the war and afterwards. Once, during an air raid in London, while printing in the basement of our London house, I had to pack up, as it was impossible to keep the enlarger steady because of the bombs shaking the equipment. Later I went on to even do colour processing.

CHAPTER TWO

Learning to Fly – Northolt

Learning to fly, indeed one's whole flying career, is an enjoyable process marked by particular flights which stand out above the others.

The initial flights up to first solo can never be tiresome, though they can be a little alarming. I was very lucky in my initial instructors; the Chief Instructor of the University of London Air Squadron (ULAS) was Wing Commander T.F.W. Thompson, who gave me my first air experience flight at Northolt. A slight eye defect did not prevent him from being a very skilful pilot. This flight was in an Avro Tutor. To my lasting regret I missed starting on the historical Avro 504, which the Tutor replaced by about a fortnight. However, I did see the Hucks Starter in action, that remarkable device, mounted on a chassis which, with the aid of a chain driven flexible drive could engage into the dog on the propeller and rotate it, turning the engine over. This vehicle always seemed to be the first to arrive at the scene of an accident. It was as if the Hucks and its drivers were imbued with unfailing optimism to apply a sort of aeronautical kiss of life to a shattered aircraft.

Our new Tutors were not then fully cleared for aerobatics. That first flight in a service aircraft was a major event for me, in spite of my previous five shillings flight experience and other short flights in civil aircraft. There was all the preparation, the fitting of the parachute, the introduction to the Form 700, and above all perhaps, roundels, and to actually handle the controls.

I was afterwards taken in hand by a series of instructors as continuity was not always easy, one had to book ones lessons to fit in with studies, but most of the groundwork was done by Flight Lieutenant J. W. ('Baldy') Donaldson and Flight Lieutenant John Grandy. One day in the Northolt circuit, 'Baldy' saw a Heron and pursued the bird around the sky. The Heron, which as any birdwatcher knows, is an adept flier, especially when avoiding attack by other birds, it probably enjoyed the exercise as much as 'Baldy'. John Grandy, prominent in the Battle of Britain and later Chief of the Air Staff, was one of the least pompous men one could meet, he was a superb pilot and instructor. I think it was he who, early one morning on a weather test, landed and took off on the comparatively new dual carriageway of Western Avenue, on the south side of the aerodrome. Then there was Sergeant (later Squadron Leader and Chief Flying Instructor (CFI) of Air Service Training) G. C. Webb and our CFI Squadron Leader H. A. Hamersley MC. It was the latter who introduced me to spinning. I was more exhilarated than alarmed by this, but was scared at the thought of doing it myself. But Hamersley – a World War I veteran and of a rather stern reputation – was an ideal instructor. He just calmly persuaded me to go through the drill of locking the slots, turning this way and that to see that all was clear below, then throttling back, raising the nose, and as the airspeed fell away and the nose dropped, to kick on full rudder. The familiar fast rotation of the ground beneath began; then there was the relief of the recovery. Climb up and repeat. I think that his manner on this flight did much to help me a few years later when I became an instructor myself and had to help nervous pupils.

We had other instructors, Sergeant Craigie, and one with whom I never flew, Flight Lieutenant G. C. Bartlett, who, with J. W. 'Baldy' Donaldson, used to do the instructor and pupil act at Empire Air Day Displays at Hendon. Superb flying with a lively and effective commentary, even in those days of none too reliable air-to-ground radio. On one occasion (a rehearsal), they were upside down at rather a low height and contrived to switch the engine off. Over the loudspeakers and all over the Northolt/ Ruislip area came a voice saying 'God, I've switched it off!' Fortunately they restarted and the show went on. All these were excellent pilots; modest to a degree and examples of all that was best in the pre-war RAF, providing the leaven which made the service great in the war years, and to this day. Alas, J. W. Donaldson was lost after the Norway Campaign when HMS *Glorious* was sunk.

Finally one day, after the familiar train journey from Marylebone to Ruislip Gardens, the day of my first solo arrived. It was also the first solo day for Tony Simpson (nicknamed 'Ernest' because of Mrs Simpson's, later the Duchess of Windsor's former husband). We reached the solo point after joining the squadron together and doing about the same number of some seven dual hours. Today, forty-one years later, I can recall little of the flight, except of an initial swing on take-off, which I more or less controlled (avoiding flying directly over the ULAS, or more correctly, Station Flight hangar) and my feelings on landing which were of agreeable surprise at the success of the expedition. In between was that feeling of being entirely on one's own in the aircraft, a mixture of delight and a little apprehension. There was no ceremony, but an incredible feeling of elation as we sped back to Marylebone from Ruislip Gardens. Life could never be quite the same again.

That first solo was to be the last flight before our annual camp, which in 1937 was at Halton, where some polishing up dual flights took place before another solo flight. Halton, with its magnificent Mess – we lived in tents in the garden – was smaller than Northolt. Looking at my logbook, it seems to me that I cannot have been a very promising pupil, the rate of dual to solo shows this. At Halton we were to see a Bulldog two seater trainer version of the single seat fighter, a Bristol Fighter and for ULAS use, the Hawker Hart trainer. Several of the senior ULAS members went solo on this (or the Hind trainer), but this was not to be my good fortune, either in 1938 at Duxford, or 1939 at Thorney Island, nor when I spent time at Sywell.

Early in the autumn of 1937 I made what might be called a 'dare' flight, although no one put me up to it. Armed with less than eight hours solo to my credit, I decided not to carry out the forty-five minutes of solo steep turns and forced landing approaches for which I had been detailed, but to fly over the centre of London instead. My target was Oxford Circus, or more precisely, the Regent Street Polytechnic, where I fondly hoped a particular friend might be an impressed spectator of this daring exploit. The method of navigation was based on elementary principles i.e. simple use of the compass, combined with a fair knowledge of the railway system of north-west London. I had Sheet 3 (1/4 inch scale) and a general street map in a directory in case of complete disorientation. Eventually, I climbed to some 4000 ft, feeling very lonely, and made my way to Oxford Circus. London from the air is even now an impressive sight to me, but to me in my single engined biplane, it was most frighteningly impressive. I made a dubious steep turn or two over Oxford Circus and then made my way back to Northolt without overstepping the time in the Flight Authorization Book. This expedition was foolish, but with the good visibility was within my capability. Although a forced landing through engine failure in Hyde Park would have been hard to explain, if successful, which it might not have been. This is the sort of act which many a young pilot used to do. The Soviet test pilot and author, Mark Gallai, has written about the early days of the great pilot, Valery Chkalov, when he flew under a bridge over the Neva (and under high tension cables) at Leningrad. It was just one of those 'dare' type flights which he just had to do to prove to himself that he could do it. At the time I was unaware of Chkalov's exploits, but like Chkalov – and here the resemblance ends. I also flew under a bridge, the old railway bridge over the Severn at Lydney, and high tension cables several times later on when at about the same stage of experience as Chkalov. My bridge was much easier than Chkalov's, but it was the 'done' thing at the time. I was a bit alarmed once to see a Beaufighter coming the opposite way – I gave way! So many people flew under the bridge that a special order came out banning the practice. But I shall return to the subject of this sort of activity later.

As well as ULAS, Northolt was the home No.111 Squadron, the first squadron to get the Hurricane and we used to watch with envy. We saw one forced landing after an engine failure on take-off, which was skilfully executed with the minimum of damage. Then there was the flight by Squadron Leader Gillan from Edinburgh to Northolt, at a then incredible speed of 408 mph.

Gradually time moved on and the start of the war was a bit of an anticlimax. My parents were people of strong faith and viewed the oncoming storm with composure. I got my fifteen foot boat up from the sea front, prepared some blackout, stuck paper strips on the windows and made a little brick shelter in the cellar for my collection of aircraft negatives. I had thought that I would be 'embodied' in the RAFVR before 3 September 1939, but in the event, I had to wait a few days. During the Munich Crisis the year before, I had been learning to drive in a vast Daimler Taxi with the Rev. Beauford Haste. With many people wishing to leave Felixstowe, my 'L' plates were removed and I took several parties to the railway station. Just as well they were not to know of this, but later I had to switch to a Ford 8 for my test and fail it, lamentably. Back to the bicycle until 1949, save for the holding of an Isle of Man provisional licence for a month; an emergency drive in a service car at night in the Shetlands and the droit-de-seigneur driving an RAF truck in the Murmansk area in the same year. However, at this time in 1939 there was no call for my services on the taxi. The first air raid warning and all clear came soon after Mr Chamberlain's broadcast, followed by rumours of all kinds of air activity. Soon, with the initial attacks by our squadrons, one suddenly had to accept the fact that losses to our aircraft were inevitable. This was a blinding glimpse of the obvious, but it was one of the first lessons of the war and for some reason quite an unexpected shock.

Anyhow, along came an instruction to report on 07 September to No.9 Flying Training School at Hullavington. On my way through London I called in at Plumbs in Victoria Street and ordered my uniform – the whole thing, two sets, with greatcoat and shirts included, was at a cost of much less than £50. For some years I kept the bill, but through ill luck I have now mislaid it.

Hullavington railway station was little more than a halt on the rather lesser used branch line via Badminton; it was more normal to go to Chippenham and take a taxi. But I changed trains at Swindon with time to wait for lunch and also I thought I had better open a Post Office account. In the office, the Sub-post Mistress asked about any other account and, of course, I had to declare that I had left my other book at home. She was worried about this, questioned me and said "I think you should go straight back home to your Mother". This advice I could not take.

CHAPTER THREE

Hullavington – Jurby – Upavon (CFS)

At Hullavington there were Airspeed Oxfords, Avro Ansons and Hawker Harts awaiting us. My fellow course pupils were a very varied lot in both flying and life experience and I was the youngest. While at Hullavington, there were still in residence the last peacetime course of acting Pilot Officers, these in their last few weeks of training. Our course included ex-airline pilots and operators; the officers included Reserve of Air Force Officers (RAFO), some ex Air Squadron and RAFVR, while the NCOs were RAFVR or Class D reservists who corresponded to the RAFO. One of the senior instructors was Christopher Clarkson from the aircraft side of Shell Aviation (later to play an important role in the purchase of aircraft from the USA), while one of our course was John Longley (RAFO), also from Shell, who was to become a good friend. There was an RAFVR pilot officer, who, as an Eton biology master, had earlier in 1939 done some flying practice on our ULAS Tutors at Northolt. This was Christopher Hartley, son of Sir Richard Hartley, and later to be Air Marshal Sir Christopher Hartley. His experience of the world was already wide and to be envied, with expeditions to Svalbard (Spitsbergen) and Borneo and a record – through a reference in a lecture to the properties of methylene blue – of having turned the urinals of Eton blue for a period. He and I were to team up in the Advanced Training Squadron. One of our sergeant pilots was a witty lawyer and, from my point of view, an envied and skilled operator of a Contax camera. He was later to become His Honour Peter Bristow and whose report on Dock workers was to impinge on my work in Customs & Excise some thirty or more years later. There was Christopher Foxley-Norris, now Air Chief Marshal and an erudite writer on air strategy, from whose room next to mine would come the strains of 'My heart belongs to Daddy', his waking contribution to the sounds of the early morning in the Officers' Mess. Within only a few weeks, as the APOs course finished, we were joined by another course which included two other ex-ULAS friends, Douglas Bruce and Tony Simpson (later both were lost on Hudsons), an Oxford man named Leonard Cheshire (later VC) and another from Oxford, Mr Henry Melvyn Young, a rowing man who with others brought an atmosphere of the great university to the place. Later, he was to row his crew home to safety in their dinghy after ditching on operations and, later still, he was to be one of the lost heroes of the Dam Buster's raid. Oddly enough, Leonard Cheshire, like most of us, did not seem to be as concerned with the future as with his spare time activities. For some reason or another none of us seemed to be living entirely in reality – these were the days of the 'phoney war'; we just did not know what might lie ahead.

However, no time was lost in getting our training started. The course was divided into twin and single engine groups and I, as I hoped and requested, fell into the former. The Oxford was not the easiest twin around to fly – or rather that was the view then held; later I was soon to get to like it and the precision with which it could be flown. Within a few days, while waiting to take-off, I watched with my instructor as one of our course, on his first or early solo, had an engine fail as he was coming into land. We saw the yaw, then, as he put power on the live engine to reach the airfield, the wing began to rise, up and up, and then the whole aircraft turned onto its back and crashed into the wood on the edge of the aerodrome – there was no fire. We took off for our lesson and as we flew over the scene on the approach there was the ambulance, a fire tender and the bits of broken aircraft and a lost life.

A few days later – although all were now solo on the Oxford – to our rather general relief, we received the gentler and less demanding Anson in place of the Oxfords. The hand-pumped flaps and hand-operated undercarriage are now legendary as Herculean labours and the latter was only retracted for cross-country flying.

The single engined members of the course had their Harts and Audaxes; some had already become proficient before the war had started on the Hart or Hind trainer and they had fewer problems, although one of the course was killed on a navigation exercise. They were disappointed not to have Harvards – even though these had a rather alarming reputation – or the newer and spectacular Miles Master, whose arrival on the scene in prototype form had been one of the excitements of pre-war days. It was a really beautiful aircraft, later to be developed into the less beautiful Mk II and III and the Martinet target-towing aircraft.

There was a Maintenance Unit at Hullavington and aircraft of small and medium sized types were continually arriving or departing to squadrons. One day when I was in the Control (watch) Tower as Duty Pilot under instruction, two Tiger Moths arrived. The occupant of one aircraft got out, unwisely, for his engine was still running, and went over with his map to his friend and there was gesticulation and discussion in the centre of the airfield. Finally, one of the party gave way in resignation to the argument of the other, they taxied back downwind and took off, never to be heard of again. No doubt they reached their destination. England was already dotted with airfields, and Kemble, Aston Down, Hullavington, Colerne and Lyneham were all close together, they had grass covered hangars with maintenance units attached. It was not always easy to know which was which and it was about this time that the legend arose of the pilot who walked into the Watch Office and straight up to Daily Routine

Orders, on their clip on the notice board, to confirm where he had landed!

That winter, Hullavington acted as a temporary base for the Harvards from No.6 FTS at Little Rissington, a few miles up the Fosse Way, which was snowbound at the time. This invasion was viewed with some alarm, as these particular short-service pilots from Little Rissington were allegedly a law unto themselves, but, beyond imparting some new songs and tunes to add to our repertoire and to collect some from us, they did little to disturb the calm.

Eventually, we reached the stage of so-called height tests and I had at last to fly higher than I had cycled in 1935 over the Gross Glockner Strasse in Austria. Night flying followed. My first night solo was notable for me for the sudden disappearance of the comparatively visible sight of the flare-path (the various ways of covering paraffin flares were yet to come later on in 1940). A quick flash of the landing light showed a strong snow flurry which had cut off my vision, it soon was flown through and the flare-path reappeared.

Not long after this we went into the Advanced Training Squadron (ATS), where we were to learn bombing (on the camera obscura at Kemble), air gunnery with camera guns over fields, which later became Long Newnton on the Fosse Way, and photography. In addition we were to continue with night and instrument flying, reconnaissance and similar exercises. The whole course should have been completed with a visit to an armament practice camp, but, except for a few of the single engined course who went to Penrhos or Warmwell, this was left out because of the weather hold-ups we had suffered. In the ATS we were left very much to our own devices. Christopher Hartley and I set up an enormous line-overlap record by not confining our vertical aerial photography to 20-30 exposures along the Fosse Way, we covered the length from Bath up past Kemble. Misunderstanding our instructions we each used up a whole magazine of film and each resulted in a spectacular roll of pictures.

A reconnaissance exercise in appalling weather, with the target selected by Christopher, led me to navigate him to the Man of Cerne Abbas, a landmark of which I, in my innocence, was not aware. Our ATS instructors were kindly men, more addicted to playing cards in the Flight Office, who sent us out in all weathers. One had been captain of a Whitley crew on early leaflet raids and we had many questions to ask him about the life on operations.

All through both Intermediate and Advanced training, we were engaged in ground studies which included the Link Trainer, navigation and the various mysteries of the armament world, including the concept of the Ideal Bomb – that anachronism for any recipient of a bomb unaffected by anything but gravity, its mass and velocity of release. There was also the Signal Mortar. One of the checks of this 'weapon' – which was used to effect a general recall of all aircraft flying within visual distance of the airfield (there was no R/T) by firing it from a rather revered cannon near the Duty Pilot's hut or Watch Tower – was to check the projectile both ways up, for easy fitting. Why this should have been necessary (save to avoid a disastrous explosion in the mortar) was obscure, surely it must have been made precisely? But the Sergeant was adamant, "You must test it for fit – if it fits, it fits; if it don't fit, then you're all to buggery!" We accepted this clear, simple rule as logical, but the subsequent action was never revealed. To the Sergeant's discomfort, we ensured that the Signal Mortar was included in our oral examination by the Armament Officer, who was supported at the table by our Sergeant. He, poor man, as second examiner, wriggled in embarrassment beside his superior as each of us in turn repeated the words that he had so carefully taught us. Later, all was put right when we explained that it was all a joke and poured pints of propitiatory beer into him.

We were rather less charitable to our Navigation Instructor, Flight Lieutenant Kent, who, in teaching us map-reading and map references was a little impatient with us. He would call Wisbech 'Wisbeck'. On a request to elucidate what would be found at a set of coordinates, he had to inform us that it would be 'Kent's Bottom', which physical feature was happily on the map sheet we were using for the lesson. Nor were we very happy with our PT Instructor – we would contrive to avoid his classes and were unimpressed by his cricketing record – for once he sent us off on a cross-country run in filthy weather and instead of accompanying us, merely checked us past turning points from the comfort of his car. On one dreadfully cold afternoon we were even invited to play football, but soon after this the theory got around that it was more important to train us as pilots than to ruin our health, or injure us with sporting pastimes, regardless of what ideas were held then, or later, on the importance of physical fitness. What was fascinating was that those of us who had no sporting skills, training, or wish to even support the Olympic Spirit, suffered far less from being deprived of regular exercise (other than a good country walk) than did the healthy, cold shower, run-before-breakfast school.

Our spare time was more or less ill spent, but happily so. Our Padre's house was ever open to us – John Longley and his wife lived there. 'Tubby' Guymer had been one of the first to install blackout in a church, he was Vicar of Stanton St Quintin, as well as Padre of RAF Hullavington. He himself had wished to serve as aircrew, but was unfit. He was the first of many excellent Padres whom I was to meet in my service, both during the war and after. They surely, but unobtrusively, helped everyone and never lost respect by trying to become popular by lowering their standards. 'Tubby' and Joan his wife, had two Bull Terriers, Sally and Bonzo, with whom I had many an enjoyable walk.

The winter of 1939-40 was a fierce one. One night coming back from London in a much delayed, blacked out train, I had to walk from Chippenham to Hullavington long after midnight with an airman who was also stranded, no chance of any taxi at that time and in the snow. We were nearly frozen, but when we reached the Guard Room a cup of tea made us feel almost normal again. Daylight next day showed everything, including individual blades of grass covered with a layer of ice and we did not fly for nearly a fortnight. One night when we were down to go night flying, it was so cold that after numerous attempts to hand start the Anson's Cheetahs over a period of three hours, we had got only two engines started and each of those in different aircraft! It was then decided to give up for that night.

Eventually we completed the course and said farewell to Hullavington. A final party at the Cross Hands in Old Sodbury (not for some reason at our more usual pub, the White Hart at Ford) and we were on our way. Christopher Hartley and I were sent to Jurby on the Isle of Man to fly air gunners around. On the way over, the ship was 'shot-up' by a Jurby Blenheim. At Jurby we were to put in as much flying as possible – there were Blenheim I's and Hawker Henleys there – I had a total of 230 hours, fifty-four solo on single engine aircraft and seventy-eight on twin engine (of which two hours twenty were night flying); all the rest was dual. So I needed to get some time in before going a month or so later to the Instructor's course at the Central Flying School at Upavon. Christopher had other ideas and managed eventually to get on to some ferry flying and went to Upavon later; but he was at Jurby all the time I was there. Some twenty-three years later, Jurby was to be the first station to which my daughter, then in the Womens Royal Air Force (WRAF) was sent to after her training!

We had a lot of pleasant times on the Isle of Man in 1940, hill walking and motoring about the place. Jack Bellingham and I shared a £5 car, first an MG, then when that proved a bit worn out on test, we went over to some rather less racy model which had a way of shedding its battery through the floor, but it lasted us out. We also did some fishing, or rather acted as ghillie to Christopher. We had magnificent teas at the Sulby Glen Hotel, followed by beer there, or in Ramsay. My batman had been to St

Petersburg with some military mission in the first war and had had a meal sitting next to Rasputin. Rasputin passed him the butter, "But I didn't feel like taking any! He was a fearful looking man!"

One night when I was Orderly Officer, we had a practice attack alarm. I was expected to hurry over to the WAAF Quarters to keep them under guard against possible marauders taking advantage of the situation. I raced the shortest way from the Officers' Mess across the fields and ran full tilt into some barbed wire. Not surprisingly oaths followed and I made my way round, which took quite a time.

"Is all in order?" I asked.

"Yes," was the answer, "but we're glad you've come as there was someone trying to break through the barbed wire a few minutes ago and he was swearing terribly when he found he couldn't get through!"

At Jurby, Christopher and I flew the Blenheim I, while a new friend, Jack, (with whom I shared the car) was on the Henleys. The Blenheim was a delight in many ways, although a completely failed airspeed indicator on my first solo on type was a useful experience. The Blenheim was, however, a stable aircraft which one could trust and we got down all right. Our job was to take up pairs of air gunners who shot at sleeve targets towed by the Henley pilots. At times we got pretty close to the targets to help the gunners. I remember one, who, on his first flight, got his parachute harness upside down, which was no mean feat. Across on the Scottish Coast to the north was West Freugh, where similar work was done with Handley Page Heyford biplanes and one Pilot Officer Mostyn Brown achieved fame by having to bale out of his Heyford with his gunners. I forget the circumstances but he was to turn up later at South Cerney.

Soon Jack and I were on our way to Upavon for our course. Upavon was the historical home of the Central Flying School

(CFS) and in 1940 combined the instructor courses with special conversion courses for Air Transport Auxiliary (ATA) ferry pilots, senior service pilots in need of refresher flying and various other functions. Again we were divided into single and twin engined groups, although all of us had to do the elementary instruction patter course on the Tutor. Jack was on the single engined course. Ben Crawley, whom I had had as an instructor at one of the pre-war annual camps was my instructor here and he was a master of the art. We used the comparatively level north airfield occasionally, but mainly the very undulating main airfield, even for night flying. During our time, a Short Stirling came in one day and we also saw the meeting of a captured Me 109 and a Gladiator (flown by 'Baldy' Donaldson) in mock combat. Some of our solo flights, or rather flights with fellow students representing a pupil (as at Hullavington on gunnery exercises), involved low flying and there was nothing like one's fellow students' efforts to really scare one. But the main purpose of those flights was to practice the instructional patter. Life in the Mess at Upavon was still of a very high order, with excellent service, silver plate and unforgettable curries, as well as the beautiful evenings of the early summer of 1940, before Dunkirk brought everyone down to earth. Ben Crawley used to enjoy forced landing practice at a field near Marlborough; I think he despaired of my aerobatics, which had already been commented on by a CFS visiting team to the ULAS camp before the war. A. H. Donaldson, one of Baldy's brothers, remarked "Well, you did that roll, but how you did it, heaven alone knows." I was never any good at aerobatics, but got some satisfaction out of loops and especially a roll off the top.

CHAPTER FOUR

Instructing – Little Rissington and South Cerney

Finally the CFS course was over; no one passed out with any exceptional rating and we were all distributed around the Flying Training Schools. In the interval between the end of the course and reporting to my new station I was married (to Bee) and moved up to No.6 FTS at Little Rissington, now mainly an Anson FTS, but there were also some Harvards. The old ITS/ATS division had vanished and pupils went to Operational Training Units (OTU's) for their applied flying and conversion to operational types of aircraft. My instructional career began with the sky full of blackish haze from the oil fires at Dunkirk; there was frequent over flying of the midlands by German aircraft and sporadic night bombing.

Although based at Little Rissington, Bee and I lived with our Aberdeen terrier, Sally, at the Lamb Inn, Great Rissington. I flew daily to either Kidlington, north of Oxford, or to the landing ground at Windrush, to the south. At Kidlington we were accommodated in tents about the airfield and it was here that I first met Polish airmen and contact began with that country in which I was eventually to serve. We arrived one morning at Kidlington to hear an aircraft passing overhead – it was a Dornier on reconnaissance.

Various measures were taken, after night flying we had to do a dawn patrol over certain areas to check for any signs of parachutists. What the local people thought of this exhilarating low flying, I cannot think. One evening, being alone with Sally at the Inn, I took her with me over to night flying at Kidlington in the Anson, contrary to King's Regulations and Air Council Instructions. On the anti-parachute patrol back in the early morning she sat on my passenger's knee and enjoyed the flight, barking at the cows in the field – in much the same way as after the war, she was to bark from the top of the cliffs at Unst at a great whale coming up far beneath!

At this time we received revolver holsters – but no arms. I remedied this by carrying my old Webley air pistol as the least I could do to contribute to the country's defence. After the Dornier incident, we suddenly received a Spitfire. This was to be used if any German aircraft again appeared over us. But first we each had to fly it. Lots were drawn for this and one of the flight commanders was to have the first flight, to my surprise I drew the next turn. However, the flight commander burst the tail wheel on landing, and while awaiting its repair a telephone call came through – our Spitfire was needed urgently at a squadron in Kent and it was not to be flown before collection. This was my negative contribution to the Battle of Britain.

Our pupils progressed gradually and our life was enlivened by such things as the occasion when two Ansons collided on landing in the centre of the aerodrome. We had no radio or even visual means to warn them. We ran to the scene – it looked as if there must be at least one casualty – expecting to find people needing succour, but nothing of the sort! The two occupants, enraged with, and blaming each other for spoiling their respective landings, were slogging it out with their fists beside the wrecks. Another pupil, with the invariable flap trouble of the Anson – blowing into the up position because of too high a speed, or a faulty valve – sailed across the airfield towards our tent, overshooting, for his landing. Telepathy, to tell him to take off again, did not work, even with the various adjectives added for good measure. He demolished our tent with its tables and tea things, but mercifully our timekeeper had just left the tent. We gazed at the scene of confused canvas and aircraft for a moment in horror and then Bill Nathan, our flight commander, walked up and in a great moan said, "My Gad, his wheel has gone over my best tunic!"

Night flying at Kidlington was a bit tricky, especially when it was very dark, but our comrades at the Hampden OTU up the road at Upper Heyford had fairly frequent crashes and the apparently inevitable fires which resulted – whatever tragedy may have occurred – gave us illumination to get a visible horizon and something (we always thought it was the magnesium alloy wheels) seemed to burn for a long time. The darkness had its compensations. I was the recipient of a thoroughly undeserved rebuke from one of the other flight commanders in the dark. He turned away to walk off and disappeared into one of the rather deep air raid shelter trenches. Poetic justice!

Windrush had a major event one night, 18 August 1940, when a Heinkel 111 flew over the flare-path and then came back to shoot at an Anson, which I think, was coming in to land and was going around again having received a 'red', telling it not to land. Suddenly, there was a big explosion just upwind of the aerodrome and fires on the ground. It was assumed that this was the Anson, but those running to the scene across the stone walls and fields found no trace of the Anson. The fire was from the Heinkel which had blown up, while further on lay the unburnt Anson, wrecked, with its pilot dead. Witnesses said that they considered the Anson pilot deliberately turned into the path of the Heinkel and forced a collision. There was no proof, unfortunately. The wreckage proved of great interest, as apparently one or more senior officers had been on the Heinkel, as well as its usual crew. The Station Commander of Little Rissington inspected the wreckage and saw a smart pair of flying boots; he remarked, "They're nice and about my size too." But he lost interest when it was pointed out that the late owner's feet were still inside.

"Struck off the strength, I think sir!" was Sergeant Murphy's comment on another gruesome find. I am afraid that we souvenir hunted and recovered various things of no real technical interest. I had an oxygen bottle and a parachute ripcord which I later sent to the Little Rissington Museum when CFS moved there after the war.

About this time, when flying from Windrush instead of Kidlington, we could see a Handley Page 42 (Hannibal class) of Imperial Airways a few miles away at Bibury aerodrome. This was the last time I was to see one of these aircraft, so well known to me from pre-war days 'spotting' at Croydon. On another day we saw an enemy aircraft, possibly a Ju88, swoop down over Bibury and drop a stick of bombs near their Nissen huts. Later, I was to hear more of this. At South Cerney, the parent station for Bibury, there was a small bomb disposal team and the NCO in charge became a friend, showing me his various trophies. He was to lose his life at this dangerous work. I am ashamed to say my diary does not contain his name; he was a modest man and told me about this particular stick of bombs at Bibury. Someone was sure that there was an unexploded one because of the craters and a single entry hole extra. My friend was summoned, and arrived to be greeted with great admiration by all present, who then made themselves scarce. He investigated and found that the mysterious hole was indeed the point of entry of a bomb which had hit the underlying Cotswold rock, ricocheted out and exploded further on. After his hero's welcome he felt all that he could do was to tell the nearest senior officer of the situation and said, "I quickly got back into the gharry (truck) and left the scene. It would have been too much to let down that crowd".

Meanwhile at Felixstowe there were frequent raids. Mother and Father worked at the Report Centre at the Police Station. On one occasion a stick of bombs fell by the Report Centre and an unexploded one fell by the front door. Mother reported in a letter, "we couldn't use the front door for some time," but she did not reveal the reason, nor did she mention that they had, of course, continued on duty.

One Sunday, about the time of the Windrush Heinkel incident on the 18 August 1940, while walking off duty, I suddenly heard the noise of explosions and the sound of an aircraft and saw, across the Cotswold countryside, flames and smoke rising up from Brize Norton. A successful raider had found aircraft in the hangars and destroyed many of the Oxfords with its bombs. Jack Bellingham was instructing on Oxfords there and I was relieved to hear later that he was alright. He had been taking a bath at the time, "what a place to be found dead," he said. It was estimated that from the moment an Oxford caught fire, it was less than half a minute before it was burnt out. After this loss of aircraft, measures were taken to distribute them around and near the airfields in scatter fields.

In late August came my posting to No.3 FTS at South Cerney, with HQ No.23 Group, soon to be under the command of Air Vice-Marshal Sir Keith Park on rest after the Battle of Britain. Here, I was to be instructing on Oxfords and usually flying daily over to the 'relief landing ground' of Bibury. Each flight had a flight lieutenant as flight commander, with a senior flight lieutenant overseeing two flights as 'group commander' – he was responsible for doing tests. We operated on a shift basis, so he also gave some continuity. One flight would normally be operating from South Cerney and one from Bibury. The first day, I was flown over to Bibury, did some instructing and then came the end of the shift and the need to return to South Cerney. One Oxford had an unserviceable airspeed indicator (ASI) and our group commander, as the most experienced pilot, should, I think still, have flown it back. However, he did a fine bit of delegation and I was given the task and a lot of free advice. But, after the ASI failure on the Blenheim at Jurby, I was confident about this and the flight passed off without any difficulty; the Oxford could be nicely trimmed to settle down at the correct angle of approach.

These ferry flights to and from Bibury were used in various ways, sometimes for particular work with pupils, more often an occasion for instructors' formation flying. Sometimes other instructors would take over from their pupils and demonstrate some feat of aviation, or go to look for – and at – the latest local bomb crater from the air. The feats of aviation sometimes included aerobatics.

Life at South Cerney has been in many facets well and accurately described in the book "*Yellow Belly*" by John Newton Chance, so I will dwell on other aspects of life there. Night flying at Bibury was a tricky operation. The goose neck flares (sort of watering cans with paraffin in the can and an enormous wick from the spout) now covered by a sheet metal cover which rendered them almost invisible to us as well as to the Germans, unless flying very low. The electric glim-lights were also pretty dim, but Bibury was a grass, bumpy field, on the top of a hill plateau right in the middle of the country, giving the blackest nights anyone might wish for or wish to avoid. There was no horizon at all and hill fog would often creep in suddenly without much warning. I was once caught out in low cloud and hill fog on a weather test, but managed to get back. On another occasion the fog rolled in when a pupil was up on his first night solo. I was on flare-path duty at the time and with the airman helping me, took off the covers; we overturned all the flares and threw Very cartridges into the blaze. The whole conflagration made such a noise and with the fog as well, the airman and I did not see or hear the aircraft land. Another airman came running out from the huts to tell us that it was down, just as our final Very cartridge went off and the flare flew towards him, causing him to leap high in the air as it passed between his legs! "It's landed!" he shouted.

On another occasion a pupil, caught out by fog, found a field free of fog in moonlight on ground higher than the airfield and skilfully landed his aircraft intact using his landing lights. Enemy aircraft occasionally shot up the flare-path at Bibury or again at

Windrush, for this we were given a machine gun to ward them off. Eventually, even this was taken from us, there was always a great rush to be the one to fire it and sometimes we had an RAF regiment man on duty to do so. On one occasion, the gun was fired in anger at a raider by a visiting regiment officer who claimed, to our undisguised scepticism, that he had scored a hit.

We were granted one aid, the siting of a neon flashing beacon (coded) some two or three miles from the field and a pair of 'leading lights' positioned about a mile upwind to give a rough horizontal reference in the tricky moment between leaving the flare-path and getting decently airborne and on instruments. A Chance floodlight was also available for emergency illumination of the landing area, but it was not often used, as in mist it made things worse and because it would attract enemy aircraft. Similarly, minimum use was made of landing lights. All this did not prevent frequent accidents, some minor, but any major ones were almost always fatal. Fatalities being more frequent than minor injuries and with the shortage of medical officers (MO), there was no Duty MO at Bibury, though there was one at South Cerney, half an hour away by ambulance.

New arrivals, certainly instructors, were 'encouraged' by tales of grisly finds among wreckage, such as an escape axe in the dead instructor's hand, apparently having been used in a desperate attempt to cut his pupil's hands from the controls on which they were frozen in fear! I was to get into a situation by having a pupil raise the undercarriage when we became unstuck prematurely on a night take-off over the rough surface. It all happened very quickly, we sank back, the wooden propeller tips broke off, the engines over sped and there was nothing that could be done but throttle back, abort the take-off, switch off – and hope! We slid along the ground and hit the boundary wall, solid Cotswold stone, at about 70 mph. The aircraft disintegrated and I got a blow in the face and leg. My pupil was unhurt and after releasing our harnesses, we staggered through the wreckage to the back door which I solemnly opened and was greeted by an airman, "Are you alright sir?"

"Yes," I ungraciously replied, "just go and start up another aircraft!" And I fell at his feet, flat out. In fact the aircraft was so effectively smashed that we could have walked out straight from our seats at the front. I can recall the kind concern of my fellow instructors and the pupils, including Peter Horsley, at my injuries, but also in my moments of semi-consciousness, I realized that there was equal concern as to who was to be the lucky instructor to have my night flying bacon and egg as well as his own. No doubt I would have shown the same concern, if I had been in their position!

I was taken back to South Cerney where the duty MO said, "What a nuisance, you're the first to survive a night flying prang for months, I suppose we will now have to do duty at Bibury!" He put stitches in my face and received an appropriate comment on his work from me, which at least the WAAF nursing orderly appreciated. My cut leg and the fracture under my bruised cheek were left to be dealt with at Yatesbury Hospital, to which I was removed the next day for a fortnight.

Next morning Sandy Barker, our senior MO, and an excellent pilot himself, came and saw me and said he did not think much of the stitching, "Pity I wasn't on duty!" Our chief instructor also came along and commiserated, saying it was not my fault.

After Yatesbury, I had a fortnight's sick leave in the Scilly Isles (to be repeated the next year when I got contagious jaundice in a village epidemic) and then back on duty. The Germans were active around the Scilly Isles and we recovered a dead fisherman from the water on one trip. Later, the small De Havilland Dragon that took people to and from the mainland, was shot down by marauding aircraft between the Isles and Penzance. By 1942 there was a Hurricane flight (at least one aircraft) at St Mary's and on the mainland at Predannack, near Mullion Cove, there were Beaufighters. I rode in the back of one flown by my former South Cerney flight commander Paul Elwell.

All this time in 1940-41 there were intermittent night raids on flare-paths, as well as the main attacks. We had some Hurricanes of No.87 Squadron on Bibury, flying night fighter operations as required. We had watched the German aircraft overflying South Cerney area on their way to Coventry. One large bomb had landed in Ashton Keynes village killing the occupant of a nearby cottage. Near Ashton Keynes there was a 'Q' site – a dummy aero-drome which collected quite a few bombs. On off duty walks we would find the odd burnt out incendiary bomb and one day found one unexploded, caught by its tail in wire netting. I proposed that we should throw it like a dart at a stone to set it off and then see if we could extinguish it with some nearby sand and turves, as advised. It went off beautifully as it hit the stone, we piled on the sand and (*grass*) sods and it seemed to be extin-guished when there was aloud explosion and most of it flew towards my legs and Sally, the Aberdeen, made off to home, to treat us very coldly for some days. This incendiary had been one of the first to have a small explosive charge in the tail to deter the air raid wardens – we had not heard of this modification.

On another occasion a German raider was shot down near Kemble, crashing at the Manor House at Coates (a Ju88 on 25 November 1940). Later, a former South Cerney pilot (Flight Lieutenant A. S. Pain), then on Beaufighters, shot down a German aircraft near Brinkworth.

Spring of 1941 brought new delights, not least of which were the fritillary fields near Ashton Keynes, by the very young Thames on whose banks we also lived, first at the Manor House Farm at Ashton Keynes and then down in the village with Cecil Short and his sister, in the Mill House, with trout in the river. Here, my photography got us into a little trouble when the print washing water overflowed in the bedroom and downstairs in the living room I suddenly saw a drip on the ceiling. Oddly enough it dried out completely. The Shorts were very kind to us. Our nearest railway station for leave was at Minety. I once collected a leave ticket which had to be made out on a special form. It was No.23 in the book and the booking clerk had to cross out 187 on the date and put in 1941! Later we moved to the village of Poulton where we lived in the beautiful Manor House on the Cirencester to Fairford road. Fairford was our railway station and when one arrived for the early train the steam was still being raised.

In 1941 a scheme (with a non-PC name in our modern age!) was started to aid lost aircraft – WAAF operators sat by the TR9 radio sets which had a very limited range; lost operational bomber or night fighter aircraft would call out the codeword and if they were heard, the ground operator would answer giving her position and tell the aircraft to circle until the flare-path could be lit (if not lit already) and accept the aircraft. Because of the weakness of the set, the aircraft would certainly be within five minutes or less of the ground station and could thus be heard. Our WAAFs, Sally, Ethel and Margie rescued several operational aircraft in this way.

Later, we were to have TR9 sets fitted to the Oxfords (or some of them) and we eventually started a small programme of night cross-country exercises around the local aerodromes and beacons. For this, in emergency, we would use the lost aircraft system. The opening session involved our squadron commander and one of the senior instructors. They got a trifle lost and left their TR9 R/T set on 'Transmit'. Those on the ground listening to the WAAFs set in the South Cerney watch tower with the WAAFs, were delighted to hear the several times repeated conversation from the Oxford cockpit, "Can you see the _____ flare-path, Bogey?"

"No sir, not a sign of the _____ thing!"

"Oh there it is!"

Then some confused noise and "Oh God, we've been on transmit all this time!"

CHAPTER FIVE

Aerobatics, small fields, low flying and more of South Cerney

arlier I mentioned how it was, for a time, the practice at South Cerney and nearby aerodromes to fly under the Lydney railway bridge across the Severn. This practice had largely replaced a fashion of doing aerobatics, particularly barrel rolls, in the Oxford – although one such flight earlier on had ended in disaster and loss of life when an aircraft had disintegrated in the air doing a loop. This was an activity I had no inclination, being too scared, to take part in and in any event it seemed to me unwise to strain the Oxfords, already flown and strained by many and varied pilots. Often, too, there were loose objects, metal screw pickets and heavy aircraft covers stowed loose in the back. On a re-categorization flight at CFS, an instructor showed me a loop in the Oxford. He was later to attempt a roll in a Hudson, which resulted in irreparable damage to the aircraft and severe strain and injury to himself. He had a point though, for an operational aircraft could sometimes get on its back out of control and it was less strain to roll into level flight.

34

One of the most difficult temptations to resist was early one still morning at about 2000 ft over the Black Mountains of Wales; I noticed what looked like a perfect bit of level mountain grass. There was a long enough run to get down and get off again and it would have been most satisfying to have done so – but what if it was bog?

The fascination of landing and taking off from fields and other odd places must have been originally born in me at school when I had seen aircraft landed and taken off from the far fields, beyond the playing fields, or at home, when an Avro 504 gave joyrides from a local field at Walton; how I envied my Aunt who made one such flight! We had Sir Alan Cobham and the Hon. Mrs Victor Bruce using fields at Felixstowe, now covered with houses. This interest was added to with forced landing practice training and a real forced landing in a field full of mushrooms in Sussex in 1939. In 1941, fields near some woods were prepared for aircraft storage in those woods and we used these strips for training. Such a field was Overley Wood near Cirencester.

As instructors, we were often required to pick up pupils who had made forced or precautionary landings when lost, they were under strict instructions not to attempt to take-off again themselves. On one occasion, in an Anson in 1940, I was flying out the aircraft which another instructor and myself had flown to the scene in. While he flew out the pupil in the lightened aircraft to a nearby airfield to refuel and got off fairly easily, my aircraft was heavier, being almost fully fuelled, and I caught the tail in the far hedge, bringing back a piece of stick in the tail and three broken fuselage elements.

On another occasion I was telephoned by a Canadian pupil, "I'm down by some old rocks on a racecourse near Salisbury" – Stonehenge! Another pupil landed on the uncompleted runway at Harwell. By the time we, the rescuers, got there, the workmen had obstructed the runway against glider landings and we were left with a small length of taxy track to land on and take-off from. One aircraft, which could not be flown out of the field it had been landed in, was almost on the edge of South Cerney. Late one evening we were waiting in the flight hut for the return of an Australian pupil on a cross-country navigation exercise. Suddenly, when, after no news, we were getting really worried, a figure appeared with a parachute over his shoulder coming over the hedge in the direction of the line of approach. "Hullo, X," I said, "and where have you left your aeroplane?"

"It's out there in the bush about half a mile away," he said.

One engine had failed on the approach and he had, unnoticed by anyone on the airfield, made a most skilful landing in a small field not far from South Cerney village, but he had had to walk some way to get to a bridge to cross the canal running between his field and the aerodrome, to get back to us.

Unauthorized low flying was often a cause of accidents, sometimes this low flying was done by pupils whose instructors would not let them handle the controls at low-level, they demonstrated the technique, but never handed over control to allow the pupils to practice properly under supervision. But more often, the accidents occurred as a result of bravado, born from the humdrum work, particularly of the instructors who specialized in night flying. To some it gave satisfaction, to the unlucky others it brought death. One could blame the pilots for taking the risks, but it was understandable. What was not so bearable was that it caused unnecessary loss of life, much unhappiness to wives, fiancées, girlfriends and parents, and finally the destruction of much needed aircraft.

As duty officer, one evening I was asked to come to sick quarters to identify a friend, and, perhaps his passenger, who had been killed in a low flying crash. I identified my friend with difficulty. My wife was a close friend of his and I suggested to the CO that it might make things easier if she went and broke the news to the widow, instead of one of the other officers going. He agreed and she went – I hope that this made things that little bit bearable. An unfortunate thing about this accident was the loss of a ring of particular sentimental value. It was not found on the body and the wreckage was in minute pieces scattered amongst the trees; my wife and I spent an hour or so searching the area without result.

A few days later I was discussing this crash with another pilot who made the remark, "I can't think why he did it". This man was killed in a similar accident a month or so later. Once again boredom, induced by the rather humdrum and at times dangerous work of night flying training, was probably the cause. There was added sadness, as the man was engaged to one of the watch tower WAAFs and they always heard of crashes first. One of the worst was when two aircraft on a formation exercise collided right over the watch tower and came down beside it.

Accidents always seemed to happen in threes and this superstition was frequently supported. The reason was no doubt pure coincidence, the large amount of flying and the very large number of aircraft operating, and of course, the lack of aids and direct radio control, other than a good look out in the circuit. There was little enough time for us to analyse the why and wherefore, although investigations took place into all accidents. I remember a particularly unpleasant time I spent with an investigating officer who seemed to have no idea of the pressure under which we were working. This had been a case of a mid-air collision with a fighter aircraft from elsewhere, our aircraft had an experienced instructor with a former elementary flying instructor as his pupil (on a conversion course to twins) and the fighter pilot, as I recall, was no novice. There was scarcely any question of blame that could be attributed to our organization. Navigation training was fairly elementary – map-reading and mental dead reckoning with compass and watch as the most essential aids. Once, on a navigation test, a Canadian trained pupil had to map-read his way round the Gloucester balloon barrage and then pick up a small river on the other side to complete the leg to Hereford or some town not far from there. No checking against his compass and the relative bearing, he wrongly picked the Severn, in place of the small river. As he map-read, the Severn became wider and wider. "This creek sure is getting big," he said. I pointed out the compass heading and remarked that if we had continued on that heading, once we crossed the South Wales coast there was nothing between us and South America. The lesson went home and his next effort was impeccable.

Flying was not stopped if there was an accident, unless there was no reserve fire engine available. This was a surprise for those trained overseas and I was once asked by a pupil, after we had witnessed an accident, "I suppose that's the end of flying for today?" My answer was to turn into wind, open up the engines and take-off.

One of the more trying, but necessary, annoyances was the need to park the aircraft in the 'scatter' fields around the aerodrome after flying and then walk back to the hangar, parachute etc over one's shoulder, to one's bicycle and home. Once they were proficient at taxying, the job was usually given to the pupils in the evening, but it was normal to walk out to the aircraft in the field the next morning to do the pilot's part of the daily inspection. There was no real circuit traffic control in those days and the duty pilot in the watch tower (affectionately known as "Bullshit Towers" at South Cerney, as HQ Flying Wing was accommodated therein) was usually busy on the telephone, only keeping a perfunctory visual watch. Sergeant Verdon Roe always seemed to be back first from the 'scatter' field after flying back from Bibury. The mystery was explained when we found that Verdon, no mean pilot, instead of landing on the aerodrome and taxying back via the hangars, used to land short in the scatter field instead. Quite apart from this, he used to provide us with much entertainment when the weather was bad and we were waiting for it to clear. I think the pupils were surprised to see their instructors in tears of laughter when they looked in our office from the crew room.

Among those with whom I served at South Cerney was Owen Chave, a former civil flying school instructor and a poet – and a very good poet, too. He was later to be lost on operational flying over Italy. He had contrived a way to remember the mnemonic letters for the pre-flight take-off checks, or cockpit drill, TMPFFS (Trim, Mixture (and tighten friction nut), Pitch (although we didn't have this in the Oxford, although there was a lever to touch to complete the drill), Fuel, Flaps and Sperry (gyro) instruments. Owen claimed that these letters were in themselves hard to remember and so he used to tell his pupils that they could recall the letters by recalling a phrase in order to confirm the mnemonic. Suffice to say the phrase began with the word 'tickle' and ended with 'sake'! One day he met up with a new pupil who said, "Sir, if you're going to teach me with obscenities, I'll have to ask to be transferred to another instructor."

Owen told us this with glee, adding without malice, "He'll never get far in the RAF, if he thinks like that."

His best known poem was "The Flying Instructor's Lament', but his others reflect a rather more serious side, for he was acutely aware of the issues behind the war. On another occasion on night flying, one of his false teeth shot from his plate as he was expounding some fine point to his pupils before getting into the aircraft. We beheld the scene of the three of them searching for the missing tooth. I was on my way to my aircraft at the time – I forget if they found it.

There was also Freddie Poulter; he had won the British Empire Medal (BEM) at Quetta during the earthquake. What he did was not revealed by him, although he claimed to have caused the phenomenon! He said he was servicing some recalcitrant aircraft at the time and he remarked "!*%$ and!*%$ this aircraft, I wished there'd be an earthquake!"

"And," added Freddie, "there was one".

Later he was to win the Air Force Cross for his instructing. He was a man who combined a view of life, which lacked all illusions, with one of the kindest hearts. Many a pilot in the war owed much to Freddie's patience and instructing ability. He was never condescending or looked down on his pupils' faults, but tore into any fellow or younger instructor who did so. Freddie was too old to go on operations and I think he wanted to give all the help he could to those who were. This was always a problem, as we were in the comparatively peaceful (I won't say safe!) work of instructing, preparing young men for the dangerous work of operational flying. It was very important to give them all the experience we could hope to give. Quite a few, after reaching squadrons, would bring us their aircraft on an air test, to show us what they were flying and give us a trip in the machine. Needless to say, almost all the instructors wanted to get on to operations themselves and most eventually did so. Freddie was one of those people who compel me to believe in an afterlife. He must be somewhere, with his smile and his ready jokes. Religion was not one of the subjects we talked about, surprisingly, because we discussed almost everything else. I do not know if he was a convinced Christian or not, but his attitude to life and people was such. Then I am reminded of the obituary for Bertrand Russell in which the writer wrote (I quote from memory), "God, in who he didn't believe, will have a good companion with who to converse with tonight."

'Bogey' Knights, was not the same as Freddie, though their names were always mentioned together, for their service history was similar, was another good friend. One hilarious episode took place when he went to collect a force landed pupil from White Waltham near Maidenhead. The pilot, who had taken him down there and dropped him off, soon returned. But 'Bogey' was delayed and we waited for him. The aircraft eventually appeared and he made the usual impeccable landing. Somehow, at lunch time he had met up with what he described as a French actress and he had decided to take her up for a flight in the Oxford before coming back to Cerney. She was completely overwhelmed by his aviator's skill, threw her arms around his neck at a low altitude and embraced him heartily. In the ensuing melee, the Oxford stalled, and stalled properly, a fairly hectic situation. Somehow, he recovered to normal flight and the somewhat chastened expedition returned to White Waltham, where a safe landing was made and the passenger offloaded.

At this time we were living in the Manor House at Poulton, surrounded on two sides by fields which produced many mushrooms. My bicycle was repaired by Mr Stafford who told me his son was also in the RAF. I condescendingly enquired what his rank was and was told Group Captain and that he was stationed in Washington. His son was one of the early instructors at the RAF Staff College when it was formed after World War I. Nearby, lived Major and Mrs Meredith and their family, he and I used to cycle to work together. He was a civilian accountant at South Cerney. One day we found a dead man in the ditch soon after we started off to work, we assumed that he had been the victim of a road accident. However, while I hurried on to flying, the Major went to the police and it was found that the man had been murdered the night before. The dead man and his wife had the murderer as a lodger. It was a sad case. Another very different tragedy was to happen later in the war when the mother and daughter of the Mitchell family, with whom we were friends, were killed when a V1 hit the Guards Chapel in Birdcage Walk.

There were other characters among the RAF. I was in charge of a barrack block where a corporal with Boer War ribbons lived and who seemed to us to be about sixty. A carpenter by trade, he was found the occasional job to do on the Oxfords and on general joinery, but much of the time he spent in the barrack block cleaning, until the Air Ministry realized they had called up someone too old. Then there was the 'phantom fitter', never there when he was wanted, but who successfully exchanged the worn tyres from his car (he used to sweep past me on my bicycle) for the new ones from the oil bowser.

We also had a noted Station Warrant Officer of the old school, who is said to have once asked a rather sleepy sentry, "What would you do if someone jumped at you out of nowhere?"

The sentry was not so dopey, and back flashed the answer, "I'd clout him over the head with a bit of bugger-all!"

There was Peter Kleboe, he used to make home-made fire-works out of Very cartridges on non-flying days. Once he nearly damaged one of our corporals with one of these. Peter was also a superb pilot. He was to die in his Mosquito on the Copenhagen Gestapo HQ raid, later in the war. There was Bill Williams, who used to look for likely mushroom fields in the low flying area and who later was on Lancasters and helped to sink the Tirpitz. We had the great Smith-Barry at South Cerney for refresher training; he created the CFS training system, which we were using, in the First World War. His time at South Cerney has been described by F. D. Tredrey in his biography and by John Newton Chance. He came complete with his own 'pet' Puss Moth, which he kept pick-eted close to the mess by the 23 Group hangar. He would take-off from there first thing in the morning and fly around the circuit to the flight huts at dispersal on the other side of the airfield. He would do his morning's (or afternoon's) flying and then fly back to his picketing point, for lunch or tea. Unfortunately, someone borrowed and damaged the aircraft, which was named 'Annabel'.

There was also Jo Newitt, our WAAF sergeant Link trainer instructor, who had learned to fly before the war and used to fly on the Oxford to keep in flying practice. A brash young Canadian pilot, once chided by her for his careless work on the Link, asked her what she knew of flying and got put in his place. Jo got married to one of our fellow instructors, Peter Palmer, an old friend from the Upavon course. Three of us flew down to Portsmouth and across to the Isle of Wight by steamer for the wedding. The return journey was not so easy. It was a sunny, bumpy day, the barrage balloons were down at Portsmouth, but we were hurried off, as they had to go up for an air raid warning. My two companions did not feel too well as we bucketed across Hampshire and Wiltshire. We landed back to find a new Squadron Commander to meet us. He was not too amused and it was only the intervention of our Chief Flying Instructor, Wing Commander Macpherson who said, "I authorized them to go, looks as though it was a good wedding, now go home and report for duty tomorrow." That closed the incident.

There was one story told by 'Eds' Edwards, who had been at the FTS at Peterborough. There, an Oxford with a pupil flying solo, crashed into a Bessoneau hangar and there was a strong possibility it would catch fire. People rushed to the scene and were pulling away at the wreckage in a frantic endeavour to get at the pilot. All at once – I think it was 'Eds' himself – someone noticed a figure in a Sidcot suit beside him who was looking a bit bemused at the scene, though helping a bit.

"Come on, heave at this with me, we want to get at the pilot!"

"But I am the pilot," said the bemused, shocked character, "and I have got out already!"

We had many Polish pupils at South Cerney and there were one or two Polish instructors to help with the work and any language problems. One Polish pupil had been having difficulty, because of the language problem. So Sergeant Clezszuk took him on. "How did you get on?"

Sergeant Clezszuk smiled and said, "He was bloody terrible, I've sent him solo!"

Some of the Poles were officers, some NCOs, and at first we had much difficulty in persuading the former to allow the latter to fly as first pilot on their combined navigation exercises. Sergeant 'W' was to captain the aircraft and fly it, while Pilot Officer 'Z' was to act as navigator and later vice versa. Several times the aircraft would return and we would see the Pilot Officer in the left hand seat. Eventually, we persuaded the Polish officers to accept this way of things, in which an NCO could be in command of an officer in the air, our own Army and Navy could not always understand it either. The Poles were fine natural pilots and their keenness and single-mindedness in whatever they did was an inspiration. But most of our pupils, as we became an Advanced Flying Unit, were pilots trained under the Empire Air Training Scheme, or in the USA and who needed acclimatizing to European weather as much as anything else, before they went to OTUs. One pilot, Pilot Officer Tweedie, had been trained at Habbaniyah in Iraq during the Raschid Ali rebellion and had flown operations on the Oxford!

Much time was spent on instrument and navigational flying and we made many flights with two pupils aboard, changing over at intervals. Sometimes, early in the morning, we would climb up through, and over the clouds. We would fly over Somerset, with the tops of the hills breaking through the sea of mist and low cloud, especially Glastonbury Tor, and then we would sweep back, breaking through a suitable opening and back to Cerney for a landing and another instrument take-off. Always remembering St Exupery in 'Vol de nuit' – "*C'est tres joli de naviger a la boussole, en Espagne, au dessus des mers de nuages, c'est tres elegant. Mais souvenez-vous; au dessous des mers de nuages, c'est l'eternite.*" ("It's very nice to fly by compass in Spain over the seas of clouds; it's very elegant. But remember; under those seas of clouds lies eternity"). On one such flight we met a Ju88 hurrying home at low-level, but he took no notice of us. At other times we would do one instrument take-off after another. Once, on a navigation flight on a very hot day, being very tired after night flying part of the night before, I dozed off in the hot Oxford cabin. I was woken by my pupil, "Sir, I'm lost!"

My reply was "So am I!"

But such was our familiarity with Sheets 8 and 11 of the OS ¼ inch series that I soon found us again. In fact, on Instructor's instrument flying, we would often see how long it took us to find ourselves without a map after flying for three-quarters of an hour or so under the hood, 'on instruments'.

Then one day, my requested posting to flying boats came through and I was to make the first step by going to the School of General Reconnaissance at Squires Gate, near Blackpool. Here, we would be further away from the reminders of the war, for on our leaves in London and in Felixstowe we had experienced air raids and seen our London house damaged several times. A friend in London had told us how, after a German aircrew member had parachuted down into her area of South London, he had been disposed of by the population. One of our South Cerney instructors, Sergeant Tweed, who had been forced to bale out of his Hurricane over London because of damage, had been lucky that he was identified on landing. That had been during the Battle of Britain, it was now mid 1942.

CHAPTER SIX

Squires Gate, Gibraltar and Invergordon

A week before departure from South Cerney, there was the usual 'battle day' training session for aerodrome defence, which, like 'digging for victory' and planting potatoes outside the hangars, was one of the wartime extras. Not that much grew in the topsoil-less ground outside the hangars and we mainly dug up fascinating fossil shells, like enormous cockles which made useful paperweights. This particular day was devoted to the opening of an 'assault course' – one look and I knew that here was a danger far greater than that of operational flying. In view of my imminent posting to 'ops', I was going to take no risk of missing the boat and I declined to try the obstacles, for I would surely have sprained an ankle or something equally inconvenient.

Blackpool was very different from Cirencester. Here, there was everything; theatres, cinemas and many restaurants. The course was pretty strenuous, with many lectures and flying on exercises on Bothas by day and on Ansons by night. The Botha had a poor reputation, for although built like the proverbial brick-built erection, it had given rise to tales of engine failures on take-off at the

46

factory airfields, with successive test pilots being killed as the aircraft rolled over and went into the ground. Even a failure in cruising flight was said to be difficult to cope with; however, there was a drill for that: Flight Lieutenant 'Tubby' Sunnucks, (our compass and astronavigation instructor, ex-submariner from the First World War and between the wars a bush pilot in Canada – with one leg) flew the Botha regularly and had devised a means of coping with the situation:

> The dead propeller could not be feathered and had to wind-mill, but the first need was to stop the yaw and then jettison fuel. He demonstrated that you could leave the controls with the aircraft trimmed, clamber aft to the fuel cocks, jettison and get back to your seat.

Tubby's lectures on astronavigation were a joy – invariably, as he had devised various simplifications and pro-formae, he would say, "I have even taught Glad my wife, one of the original Gaiety Girls to do astro and take a sight. You should have seen the stir on board the Atlantic liners when the officers were showing off their skill with a sextant. Up would come Glad and ruin all their showing off before the young girls."

He would also say, "I flew so much for them in Canada that they asked me, 'Sunnucks, would you like something called after you?', so I said that I thought a river would be the sort of thing, so they chose one and called it 'Sunnucks Creek', but the damned thing dried up all together the next year!"

Then there was his story of a chat with a young WAAF. "Aircrew," she said, "are the worst, and the more hours they've flown, the worse they are."

"So I said to her, you shouldn't sit here with me; I've done over 5000 hours."

As I have said, the Botha was very strongly built and the interior was very like a pre-war railway carriage, but as a flying machine with both Perseus engines running well, it was fast and by no means unpleasant to fly. On one exercise, the staff pilot offered the aircraft to me to fly, while he acted as second navigator to my co-navigator for that day. I worked with Ken Campbell, later DFC, from Australia, who became a Spitfire photographic reconnaissance pilot, as were several members of the course. We also had with us, Penny Pendergraft, an American who had volunteered to join the RAF in advance of his country's entry into the war. Very soon, Penny was to have to go to the US Navy, where he had a wide career involving war and peacetime flying, including helicopters and a period on Antarctic flying. Later he was in civil aviation.

The Bothas were not used at night – for this there was a flight of Ansons, flown by some rather desperate night flying characters who regarded our navigation efforts with probably well deserved scepticism. We were encouraged to use our astronavigation when the stars could be seen, but the main noise in the aircraft was the sound of the pilots requesting continuous updated courses to steer back to Squires Gate. The astronavigation required a lot of ground practice in off duty hours, drawing out one's calculated position lines, with the north-south coast line near Blackpool giving a good check on accuracy. It was at Squires Gate that we saw some of the first American B17 Fortresses flying over England, there had not been any in the Gloucester area and we also saw P38 Lightnings. Burtonwood was not very far away, presumably they were from there.

The course over, a few of us were kept on at Squires Gate as staff pilots, flying the Bothas on exercises and also on assorted photographic sorties – one of these involved a visit to South Cerney for lunch and to show off my Botha. A small expedition also arrived at Squires Gate with two impressed civil aircraft to give air cadets air experience. One aircraft was an Airspeed Courier, flown by Flying Officer Braithwaite, ex South Cerney and a former Tiger Moth instructor and a De Havilland DH86 four engined airliner captained by J. C. T. Downey. The Courier was fascinating, particularly as it had partially removed dual controls, meaning that you could fly the thing with hands only from the right hand seat – one hand on the control column and one working the rudder control linkage (instead of rudder pedals). It was also interesting to fly the DH86, which would occasionally have an engine failure on take-off, but at the loads we were flying it at, the effect was virtually negligible. There were also journeys on leave in this period, all undertaken in those blue-lighted, blacked out trains of wartime England.

In the end our postings came through, to No.210 (flying boat) Squadron at Sullom Voe, Shetland. We set off to go there; Ted Sleigh (formerly Warrant Officer, now a Flying Officer), Penny and myself. Travel was by train to Invergordon and on from there by aircraft, boat, or whatever was available. On arrival at the transit camp at Invergordon, some surprise was expressed that we were not clairvoyant and did not know that the squadron were on their way southwards. 'Why had we come?' – 'Because we had been sent.' Then of course, followed the usual display of wisdom and we were turned around and sent to Pembroke Dock in south-west Wales. A short period of time was allowed to wash, shave and eat before we undertook this trek. The explanation was, of course, that 'postings' had not caught up with operational moves and no one was really to blame. No doubt the wise men of Invergordon made such errors themselves at times. Anyhow, off we went to 'Little England', beyond Wales.

No.210 Squadron had completed a tour at Sullom Voe with detachments in North Russia. These months had been notable for the exploits of Flight Lieutenant 'Tim' Healey DSO, and his crew, flying several times to Spitsbergen and North Russia, on flights well up to maximum endurance of the Catalina and in some appalling weather conditions. With them had flown, as adviser and Spitsbergen expert, Lieutenant Commander R. Glen, later to be well known in commerce as Sir Alexander Glen (but I am not sure if he ever returned the flying boots which he had on loan and for which we were searching, after an enquiry about them in 1944 at Sullom Voe). The crew had included Flying Officer Martin, Flight Lieutenant Schofield DFC (navigator), Flying Officer Thomas (wireless operator), David Baird and others with whom I was to fly. 'Tim' Healey had been killed in an attack by a Ju88 in the Barents Sea and was brought into Murmansk, or rather the flying boat base of Vaenga/Grynsnaya (now Severomorsk) on the Kola Inlet. He was buried there.

Having reached Pembroke Dock, we were allotted to crews as third pilots. Except for Penny, who was now being asked for by the US Navy, apparently to his displeasure. Ted Sleigh was to join Flight Sergeant Jack Fish's crew and, as I said above, I was lucky enough to join Ronnie Martin, who had taken 'Tim' Healey's place, and so I was in a proud crew. Our second pilot was Flying Officer Witherwick. We spent the days preparing for what was coming next. We had dual instruction on the Catalina with Squadron Leader Jackie Holmes DFC, the flight commander of No.210 Squadron and with Flight Lieutenant Cooper. The squadron was now becoming very large, with several crews and aircraft over establishment (size). The Squadron Commander was Wing Commander Johnson DFC, and not all the boats and crews were selected for the next operation; which was to be a detachment to Gibraltar.

Shortly afterwards, in the new year, the big squadron was to divide into No.210 (which was to be at Hamworthy, near Poole under Wing Commander Brandon) and No.190, a new number, which was eventually commanded by Wing Commander Pat Alington, who was to come from the flying boat Operational Training Unit (OTU) at Alness/Invergordon. But for the moment, it was the main body of the old No.210, under Wing Commander Johnson, who were to go to Gibraltar and join forces with No.202 Squadron, the resident Gibraltar flying boat squadron. It was November 1942.

The flight down to Gibraltar went off well. We left late in the evening and arrived in the beautiful dawn colours of the early morning after a quiet passage through the Bay of Biscay, often frequented by German night fighters looking for British transport aircraft, anti-submarine aircraft, or aircraft like ours, on transit flights through the area. Three days after our arrival and check of aircraft, we were detailed for sorties. (These were to be in support of the big convoy bringing troops, vehicles and so on, for the North African landings – Operation 'Torch'). Ted Sleigh and I shared a room and he was off first, at about 0430 in the dark, with our crew due to go two hours or so later. However, our take-off was postponed, for Jack Fish's aircraft crashed on take-off and only he and his second pilot survived. Ted was lost. The swell coming in from the Atlantic could throw an aircraft into the air before it was fully airborne and it would fall back, burying its nose into the next swell, with damage to the front end of the aircraft, or destruction, as on this occasion when the nose broke right off and the pilots were thrown clear *(Catalina AH559/N lost on 04/11/42, crew: Flight Sergeant Fish, Warrant Officer Smith, Pilot Officer H. Bardsley, Sergeant R. Leese, Pilot Officer E. J. Sleigh, Sergeant J. B. Ritchie, Sergeant T. McL Millar, Warrant Officer J. L. R. Keough, Sergeant E. T. Jones, Flight Sergeant G. Green).*

We went off later and met the big convoy out in the Atlantic: It was coming down west of the south-west corner of Spain and Portugal, and then divided. Once that convoy was through and the landings had been made, there was even more activity at Gibraltar, with aircraft continually coming into land on the Gibraltar runway. The majority were Spitfires in desert camouflage and with the special desert intakes.

The road across the runway into Spain was frequently closed for these landings and the story was told of the donkey that was held up at the barrier. Suddenly nature took its course and along with the usual rectal contents came a large number of contraband watches destined for Spain. Certain members of the RAF in Gibraltar had passes to go over into Spain on leave, but we, being on attachment, did not receive these. There were stories of visits to 'establishments' which were apparently full of delightful experiences (19/- including tea and chocolates), but interrupted by the sellers of evening papers and hot chestnuts, who entered and hawked their wares without regard to the state of play.

Our aircraft was off Algiers at first light on the morning of the *African Campaign* landings. We saw one submarine which dived directly we turned towards it. On another occasion, out in the Atlantic we came upon one, perhaps two other submarines which also dived at once. We suspected that in this latter case refuelling or re-supply may have been taking place.

Gibraltar at this time was seething with naval activity with the big ships coming and going – HMS's *Renown, Nelson, Illustrious, Furious, Argus* and various cruisers, as well as smaller ships. One of our aircraft went missing, while one of 202 Squadron's aircraft was shot down over a convoy. A night attack and also a small earthquake, all added to the interest. There were many 'characters' of the flying boat world around, among them was Ogle-Skan, 'Bismark Briggs', Gillie Potier, Pat Smallman, let alone one Graham Dowson, who often gave a series of entertaining imitations or acts in the mess. Doug Harris, with whom I now shared a room, was also extremely entertaining company. In all, I flew on fifteen operations in this short period and then went back to Pembroke Dock in time for Christmas. We stayed at Pembroke Dock for a few weeks, I set up home with my wife, Bee, and Sally, in an undamaged house in this town, which had been the target of much bombing earlier in the war and which had been one of the earliest towns in the country to be properly planned to a layout. We had a bedroom, use of a kitchen and dining/ sitting-room. The bedroom was a bit small, but we managed, if anyone was dressing, the other would have to get into bed.

Cecil White and I, destined for Invergordon and No.4 Coastal Operational Training Unit (OTU), did some dual instruction with Squadron Leader 'Squibs' Squire. He had done much of the Leigh

Light development on the flying side and was now back on flying boats. Cecil and I went solo and then set off up to RAF Invergordon, which was associated with RAF Alness.

Invergordon and Alness, in early 1943, were a bit forbidding after Gibraltar and the gentler climate of Pembrokeshire. A series of gales seemed to sweep across from the Atlantic and elsewhere, whipping up waves on the Firth and the flying boats at their moorings were snatching at them and rocking violently. Meanwhile, the dustbin lids flew up the high street of Invergordon and back again when the wind changed. Cecil White had moved into Alness Mess, by the Dalmore Distillery. We moved into Maclaren's Temperance Hotel, which was under the control of Colina and Tina Maclaren. It was temperance by name, but that did not prevent the two sisters from having the odd dram with us. Tina was mainly engaged in the kitchen, but was no second string, appearing when some plain words were needed, although Colina was the most evident in the management field. They worshipped aircrews, but were not so keen on their wives, but were tolerant of non-flying people. We would be summoned to high tea after the others (i.e. non aircrew) had been given their main course, say, a helping of spaghetti cheese. We ate more slowly and under our spaghetti cheese would be an egg, absent from the others. Of course it was naughty, but there it was. The two sisters had many a tale of flying boat people who had lived in the hotel; in the good old days when no wives were around seemed to be the message. When I was in Norway some fifteen years later, I was asked by Tina to go and visit the graves of a Sunderland crew who had left Invergordon one morning in 1940 to reconnoitre the Oslo area and had been shot down by fighters, never returning. I made the visit and sent her photographs and a letter about the graves.

Our training went apace. Paddy Boyd, an ebullient character, a fine pilot and instructor, was in charge of Cecil and me for much of the time. But quite a lot of our time at the start was spent on gale crews. This involved three of us, a pilot, flight engineer and one other, sitting aboard the aircraft at moorings. If the snatching and jerking became excessive, we were to start the engines to ease the strain, we were also expected to pump out the bilges if there were any leaks. As we recorded winds of 70 knots or more, did stints of well over twenty-four hours at a stretch amongst showers of snow and sleet, gale-crew duties were pretty appalling and a great strain, causing violent seasickness. Several aircrew (five) and two aircraft were lost before the duties were finally given up. What had made matters worse was that the rations were 'hard' ones in biscuit tins, stored in the flight office and were often raided, leaving such delicacies as herrings in tomato sauce (an inspiring dish for the seasick). Hot drinks were a trial to prepare on the heaving flying boat. Bill McGuinty, my flight engineer and Flight Sergeant Dawson spent many uncomfortable hours on this duty. The best comment on the whole business was made by one Flying Officer Shepherd of the Royal New Zealand Air Force, when tired of our instructors' continual panic about getting us out to the duty, "God in heaven, every time a rabbit farts in Dingwall, we have gale crews put on at Invergordon!" Some of the instructors were not amused by this.

One of the visitors to Maclarens Hotel was a representative from the Consolidated Company, makers of the Catalina; he used to demonstrate the circular take-off for restricted waters, which involved going hard on one engine, round and round in a circle, then as speed and water conditions became fit, full power was put onto the other engine when nearly into wind. It was a clever trick, but not really of great value at operational loads. We used to moor up for lunch during periods of solo practice (in pairs) and then we would taxy the Catalina down to Niggs Bay 'on the step' – i.e. riding on the planning bottom at about 60 knots or just under. Once, it was Cecil White's turn after lunch to be first pilot and he was standing on the seat in his RAF peaked cap, operating the wheel on the control yoke, while I was keeping straight with the rudder. The boat was light and it was essential to have a good view as there were sometimes obstacles in the narrow stretch by

Invergordon pier. Cecil's head was right out of the hatch; suddenly I realized that we were not just on the step, but being so light, we were in fact airborne and about ten feet in the air. I looked up, Cecil's face bore a contented smile, and he was unaware of the situation. I tapped him on the knee, the smile vanished and we eased back onto the water.

Another occasion at night – and a dark night at that – might not have been so funny. Cecil was in the left-hand seat with our instructor, Stan Ebdon (an old 210 Squadron friend), in the right-hand seat, giving us night dual – for Stan the first time. I was in the cabin just behind the door. We got off the water after a fairly normal take-off and then, nearly sixty seconds after unstick, we struck the water again. It was a glancing blow, but by then we should have been 300 or so feet up and climbing. Obviously we had not settled into a proper climbing attitude after unstick and had been rushing along a few feet up, just above the sea. It certainly gave the three of us a fright and we were glad to finish our flying that night.

The wind coming down the valley and along the firth from the hills near Dingwell, and especially Benwyvis, used to give very bumpy conditions over the land to the east. One day we were on the circuit over Niggs Bay when we hit a phenomenal bump. Cecil and I, although strapped in, both hit the roof together, came down, looked at each other in our surprise and at once we were thrown up against the roof again. Noises from the cabin sent me back to investigate. Jock Brown, my rigger, had been asleep in the top bunk. Now he was lying on the floor, with quite a lot of blood about and choking fumes arising from around and below him. No time for wit. What had happened was that he had been thrown up from the bunk, cut his head on a stringer, fallen back, smashing his way through upper and lower bunks and with his weight had cracked one of the practice bombs stowed for convenience in the bilges under the bunks. (The bombs were 11½ lb stannic chloride filled ones – the stannic chloride giving off thick white smoke on impact, to show how good one's bombing had been). Anyhow, the stannic chloride was reacting with the water in the bilges and with metal. We quickly got the bomb over the side into the sea beneath and started to sluice down Jock and the aircraft.

Jock was a character – he usually contrived to fall overboard just after unmooring us when we were night flying and that, of course, meant he was taken ashore by a dinghy and got an evening off, but he was a good and loyal member of the crew on operations. He had an uncle near his home in Aberdeen, who, as Jock said, was a bit of a deer poacher and used a .30 rifle. He asked Jock if he could get him some .30 ammunition (we had .30 machine guns in the Catalina nose and under-tail guns). Jock was not, it seemed, too fond of this uncle and gave him some tracer rounds. I often wonder what happened when his uncle opened fire with his first round on one of his expeditions and the tracer bullet went flaming through the dusk towards its target!

After the war Jock wrote to me and told me how he was getting on with his work in civilian life – in the furniture trade. It seemed that he was doing very well at this; then unexpectedly I had the news that he had died suddenly.

Bill McGuinty was a treasure, normally considered far too old for aircrew work; he somehow got himself on to it. He could not only do his flight engineer work excellently, he could fly the aircraft, work the radar, was an accurate gunner and very loyal. His favourite expression when upset was, "This is the most piss-poor effort I've seen in this god-damned Air Force". That said, he would get on with the job. When the Canadian Air Force was claiming back its men and commissioning them automatically, if they were aircrew, we managed to get 'Mac' commissioned in the RAF first. More about him later. The other members of the crew which formed at Invergordon were; Flying Officer Jackson (RCAF, navigator, later DFC), Pilot Officer Wheatley (second pilot), Pilot Officer Farmer, Sergeant Toner, Flight Sergeant Curwen (later Warrant Officer) were wireless operators/air gunners and Sergeant (later Flying Officer)

Dawson (flight engineer). During our time on the squadron we flew with other and additional members of the crew, but this was to be the basic No.9 crew of No.20 Course formed at No.4 Coastal Operational Training Unit in 1943.

As at other RAF stations, we had various 'battle' days and sports afternoons. Cecil White and I avoided these and in place of the programme did various long walks. First we did a short climb of Fyrish, the hill with a folly on top, above Alness. Then we did a climb of Ben Wyvis on a fairly bad day. We went into cloud at about 200 feet and walked by compass and map to the summit, where we shared a bottle of beer on the snow-capped peak. Cecil White had his own crew, too, I will not name them here, but must record a discussion which they once had on their three main ambitions. One member brought the house down with his – first, to shoot down a Focke-Wulf 190 from a Catalina; second, be present and take an active part in the destruction of a U-Boat; then he went silent. Pressed to give his third ambition, with some hesitation, he expressed a wish to perform what might be euphemistically considered an act involving lese-majesty, under rather unusual circumstances.

After the course was over, my crew and I had a period of uncertainty as it was not decided if we were to remain in the United Kingdom, or be sent to one of the overseas Catalina squadrons. For a time we were at the overseas ferry unit at Stranraer. During a BABS (blind approach beam system) course at Leuchars, under Squadron Leader Sunnucks (formerly of Squires Gate and as cheerful and good company as ever), I was able to do some flying on some other types, including the Miles Mentor, but a former civilian B.A. Eagle could not be made serviceable. One afternoon I was asked to take a Mentor over to Donibristle, a small naval airfield near No.18 Group Headquarters, so that the SASO, Air Commodore Geoffrey Tuttle, could do his flying practice. (Geoffrey Tuttle had an important role in photographic reconnaissance taking over from Sidney Cotton and was later knighted). On arrival the Mentor's Gipsy Six engine was unserviceable. The trouble was soon put right, but I had an oppor-tunity to talk with the Air Commodore and tell him that I was hoping to go to Sullom Voe. Within a few days our posting had come through. While at Leuchars, I also had the good fortune to get a flight on the jump seat in a Mosquito PR Mark IV, which was a great experience.

So there it was – we got instructions to report to Felixstowe and to collect Catalina IB, FP 222 and to ferry it, ourselves and our kit to Sullom Voe. We had to foregather at Felixstowe, so I snatched a few days with my parents at home, while we prepared the boat, took it on charge and made an air test over Harwich Harbour and Felixstowe – the balloons were lowered for us. On 21 June, we set off to Sullom Voe, with Dave Knightley as our second pilot.

CHAPTER SEVEN

Shetland – anti-submarine patrols

We arrived in Shetland in the time of the White Nights (24 hour daylight) and the yellow flag irises; a beautiful time of year and one in which one hardly wished to go to bed, but rather sit on the flying boats at anchor and fish, up to 0300hrs. Cecil White was already up there and had been involved as second pilot with Squadron Leader Jackie Holmes in a successful air-sea rescue, with an ocean landing between the Faeroes and Iceland, to rescue a Fortress crew shot down by a U-boat. One American Navy PBY 5 amphibian (Catalina) had crashed, in attempting to land beside the dinghies, with loss of life. The open-sea landing, and the subsequent take-off, can be a most hazardous operation in a heavy flying boat. Soon after this success, Jackie Holmes left for the Air Ministry and his place was taken by Squadron Leader F. W. Thomas. The CO was Wing Commander Pat Alington, formerly of No.4 Operational Training Unit, whose place there had been taken by Dick Whittome, one of the people from Hullavington days.

After a few days of training and working up the crew, we went on two operational sorties, one with Pat Alington and one with Ted Southwell, who had come back on the operational flying after his instructional tour at Invergordon. On this second flight, we were diverted to the Faeroes, with that wonderful approach over the waterfall onto Sorvagsvatn lake. We spent the night in Nissen huts and on the next day, before leaving, went shopping in the town of Sorvagsgur. During the early days of the British occupation, the Faeroese were said to have rolled down rocks onto the huts, but now were friendly, although a large fisherman followed us into the shop where we were to buy cosmetics, silk stockings and if possible brassieres, to send back to an England short of these things. The Faeroese somehow received these goods, perhaps via Iceland from the US bases, or had stocks left over from the days before the Germans had invaded Denmark. Another good buy on the Faeroes would be a whole halibut for the Officers' or Sergeants' Messes.

It was as well to note carefully, the shapes and features and relative positions of the individual small islands of Stora and Litla Dimun (Store Dimun with its remarkable single path right up to the top from the landing place on the west side), and Suderoy, under good visibility. This could be useful, especially when there was radar silence and the cloud was low, as the islands could be forbidding. Even the location of the bird colonies and species was useful on one occasion.

It may be of interest to describe in more general terms the pattern of our operational flights. The period before such a flight began with the crew being detailed on orders as 'Next available', with three or so crews in front. Once in the next three, the aircraft letter was allotted and the crew would go out to prepare it on the slipway, or at the buoy. The purpose of this was to check very thoroughly that all was in order, water tanks full; ammunition, guns, flame floats, flares, Very cartridges, sea markers, cooking stoves, elsan, dinghies – as well as the major pre-flight checks by the crew of engines and airframe. It was often a good occasion for a practice drill – dinghy drill, especially. But we also practiced attack drills, preparation of signals and so on. This done, the crew would usually rest, although a good walk, within a reasonable distance of the camp was not a bad preparation for at least eighteen hours flying, let alone briefing time. A bit of sleep was also indicated, but this depended a bit on the time one was likely to be required to take-off. Eventually, the firm time of pre-flight meal, briefing and take-off would be known – Group Headquarters having issued the executive order – and we might be told the area to be patrolled at that time too. Of course, there were frequently changes, as reflected in one tannoy announcement, "The crew of M for Mother of 190 Squadron will eat the meal of Q for Queenie." There was also the occasion when the controller forgot the word for the letter 'Q' and instead used one which may, or may not, have produced a blush among the few female inhabitants of Sullom Voe.

The call would come usually at some dreadful hour of the night, with meals ready in about three quarters of an hour and one would dress ready for the flight. Although the Catalina could be heated, it was an unpleasant system which seemed to produce more fumes than heat and so we generally relied on being well clothed in order to keep warm. The gear one wore varied with the season, but it was always wise to have extra clothes in the event of being shot down or ditching. The sea, in spite of the Gulf Stream, was always cold. We carried no parachutes, because there was no point in baling out and scattering the crew all over the sea; baling out over land was unlikely. There were blankets on the aircraft, but, of course, parachutes could have had a use as extra wrapping. I was always aware of this need to be prepared against the cold, as one of my friends had been recovered with three of his crew in their dinghy, all dead from exposure after a successful ditching. In winter I would wear ordinary underwear, then aircrew underwear (long vest and long pants), shirt (collar and tie in a pocket with studs – you never wore these when in flight as the water could tighten the tie up and strangle you), heavy pullover, perhaps a light pullover, battle dress, Irvin Jacket (in very cold weather Irvin trousers as well) over the battle dress, silk gloves and mittens rather than leather flying gauntlets, flying boots over ordinary socks and seaboot stockings. On the head, helmet, goggles, uniform cap stowed somewhere, a silk stocking around one's neck, a balaclava available and, on top of everything a Mae West life jacket, slightly inflated to give added warmth retention. Anti-sea sickness pills and benzedrine pills (to keep awake) were at hand. I needed the former after the gale crew experiences at Invergordon and in any case, although I did not often feel airsick when flying myself, it was important not to have any qualms at all with the other members of the crew depending on one's flying. With all this clobber on, one was, to say the least, ungainly. Nowhere was this so obvious as when it was necessary to go aft to the lavatory 'facilities'. These were a bit primitive; with all the clothing on, it was all quite a performance. There was an Elsan – with a modesty screen which soon vanished – in the blister compartment and in the view of the occupants, constipation was a virtue, there was also a tube and funnel for lesser affairs. The Elsan was smelly and one Captain (Flight Lieutenant Duffield) was so appalled by that on his aircraft that he wrenched it from its moorings , opened the blister wide and hurled the offending facility into the Norwegian (or it may have been the Barents) Sea, to the surprise and dismay of the natural history of the area! So, more often (than the Elsan), one used the protective top of a flame float as a sort of mini-chamber pot, using it in the rear compartment and ditching the pot and contents through the under-gun hatch, which for us, had no warlike function (except occasionally for photography on practice bombing runs). Later, ill-advised armament staff changed the flame float and a smaller version, without the useful protective cap, appeared. Some stalwarts opened this under-gun hatch and squatted across the opening, performing directly into a sort of high altitude air/water closet; this could be a very cold process indeed. It was back to the Elsan or enforced constipation. Perhaps we should have done, as I now read what Soviet pre-war long distance flyers did – they had a compulsory enema before take-off!

Feeding on patrol was very important; little and often with frequent hot drinks (and the occasional cold orange juice when available) was the best rule and it also meant that the crew was kept alert. Those off duty (there was usually one man off at a time) cooked for the others and those who couldn't cook, soon learned to do so to the crew's standard. When I was a third pilot down at Gibraltar, I soon found myself at the stove. Catalinas were fitted with a very inadequate electric hot plate, which the Maintenance Unit at Greenock supplemented with the so-called 'Clyde Cooker' – a twin primus stove with oven. Every now and again there would be a Primus flare-up. I remember one double flare-up, on a dirty night low over the Atlantic, with overload tanks right alongside the cooker. Suddenly, the door dividing the darkened pilots' cabin from the lit-up navigator's cabin opened and there was the flickering reflection of the flames from some ten feet aft. The flames rose up towards the flight engineer's seat in the wing pylon, above the stove, but Mac or Dawson were soon on hand and got it under control. But "one of our aircraft" could have been missing – for reasons other than the enemy and no-one would have been any the wiser.

A supply of sweets, chewing gum and chocolate was also available and distributed individually. Part of the inter-Canadian strife in my crew involved my navigator Jacko's chocolate, and once, while fighting a collapsed gyro-horizon, bumps and all, I was tapped on the knee by Jacko, "Do you know where my chocolate is?" he enquired. I forbear to record my reply.

Ronnie Martin's crew had prided themselves on their cooking and no member more than David Baird, he came up to me once as I sat at the controls and asked, "Would you like a cup of shit-hot tea Sir?" I replied that I hoped that it would be a bit warmer than that. Our crew from Invergordon were also adept at producing good meals and it added much to our morale.

But enough of the domestic life, back to the preparations for flight. The pre-flight meal was eaten at the various messes and the crew would meet up outside the Operations Room; the captain, navigator and senior wireless operator, would go inside. The rest of the crew, under the second pilot, would go in the transport to get rations, cameras and pigeons, and then go down to the aircraft for the final preparations for departure, stow the rations and check them over.

In the Operations Room, the navigator, wireless operator and captain would receive the details of the task, radio procedure organization, radar restrictions, up-to-date weather forecast, intelligence, which included any U-boat position details and any news from aircraft already airborne. The meteorological briefing was most important, for although the Germans were our foe, we were often in constant battle with the weather. Our forecasters were led by Flight Lieutenant 'Prof' Graham, who knew the area well, paid great attention to – and expected good in-flight reports from – the crews, sometimes flew with us and studied his charts assiduously. He would describe exactly where we would meet fronts, and he would be right. He would give us tips on the weather which would help in how and at what height we would fly. What was more, he passed on his enthusiasm and expertise to his colleagues. We had a laugh one night when a new man, just arrived, was on duty for the first time. He had been studying some last minute information and hurried over in the dark from the Met Office, fell into a ditch, but got up, carried on covered in mud and arrived to spread his chart in triumph before us. It was a complete blank: In his haste he had picked up the wrong one.

To this day I keep a very tender spot for Met. Officers – we owed them a great deal. Written up in the Mess at Sullom Voe, some unknown poet had written;

'In some high mansion, I suppose,
The weather men confront the stars,
Giving the glass tremendous blows,
And drinking deep of isobars.'

We would say good night to the controller and his staff and walk out into the dark. Aboard the truck, with all our equipment and a kit bag full of overnight diversion kit and extra clothing and down we would go to the jetty and get into the dinghy. The ride out in the dinghy was one's first real chance of a first look at sea conditions, especially important at night. Lying in one's bed resting, one had heard the wind and quite often "fears were liars", when one saw the actual water. But still the take-off was a bit tricky, even at normal loads, and with fuller tankage – anything over the normal 1450 gallons with six 250 lb depth charges – we had capacity for 325 gallons in the four overload tanks and if these were used, then the depth charge load was adjusted to compensate. The endurance with full tanks and no depth charges could, if the weather was smooth enough, allow leaning of the mixture manually to below normal auto-lean (and there was no need for frequent resort to auto-rich) and we might reach thirty hours. Requests for mixture changes, floats up and various other directions to the flight engineer were given by light signals, using switches on the control yoke.

We would come alongside the aircraft, usually the port blister and get in. The dinghy would have approached slowly to avoid damage and rocking. The captain would be peering into the darkness to decide whether to taxy out direct, or to be towed from the buoy by the dinghy, it all depended on the wind direction and strength and position of other flying boats on the moorings.

After we had clambered aboard, usually with some imprecations, the dinghy would be waved away to stand-by, if not wanted for towing, in case it was suddenly needed. There would probably be a quick briefing of the crew on any points of interest or importance about the sortie and then the boat would be brought up on to short slip ready to start engines. On short slip, we could release from the buoy quickly once the engines were running. If they suddenly stopped, the dinghy was circling close at hand.

With all covers off, the propellers turned over by hand, the auxiliary power unit (APU) running (with a hideous noise that filled the whole aircraft); we were ready to start. Normally, the starters were inertially energized; occasionally we had to do it by handle up on the wing. There was very little clearance between the propellers and much care had to be taken when working up near them. Access to the wing was up over from the blisters, or up through the pilots' hatches; a step up on the pylon between the propellers. A hand could be lost (and was) if one waved too far aft from the pilot's hatch with the engine, or engines running. Oddly enough, one flight engineer claimed that, without thinking and without harm, he had walked between the rotating propellers.

Once the engines were running satisfactorily, the aircraft pointing in the right direction, the line was slipped and one taxyed out slowly towards the take-off point. Drogues, or sea anchors, were occasionally used for manoeuvring at this stage, and certainly when mooring up. Running up and propeller exercising was done as soon as the engines were warm enough. It was normally done one engine at a time, with the aircraft circling and meeting its own wash with a familiar bump.

At night, the flare-path was a series of four or so lights on small dinghies, with a pinnace and seaplane tender standing by in attendance. Exchange of light signals with the pinnace and all was ready. One last look out, standing up on the seat, you usually got a wave in your face which removed all drowsiness. Necessary cockpit drill done, final signal, warning hooter to crew and then line-up and power on, the second pilot then brought his hand up behind yours on the throttles and held them open to supplement the friction nut, while you gave all your attention to the controls. Water went over the cabin top for the first part of the run – you concentrated on the directional gyro for line – and until the aircraft came up onto the step you could see nothing but this water, then she would be planing and you could see out as the wipers cleared away the excess. You could then check that you were in fact running parallel to the flare-path, not that there was much you could do (except stop) if you were not. I once hit the mast of the last dinghy with the rubber nose of my port float. Acceleration continued until the moment of unstick – a run of anything over sixty seconds would suggest trouble. A swell could complicate matters when on the step, but usually at Sullom Voe we were entirely safe from swell and porpoising. Finally unstuck, signal 'floats up', climb away and soon after power reduction.

No one has described the take-off of a flying boat better than St Exupery in 'Terre des hommes':

"When it is ripe, with a movement lighter than that of picking fruit, the pilot separates the aircraft from the waves and takes it into the air."

After take-off and settling down, one would make one's way to one of our points of departure from Shetland – Esha Ness lighthouse on the west coast; Remna Stacks or Muckle Flugga lighthouse on Unst. Often by the time we got there, even on a dark night, one's eyes had got accustomed to the dark and you could see the white of the surf pounding against the rocks and imagine the sea state out in the patrol area, where no flying boat could land or even ditch successfully in the event of need, let alone take-off again. Yet, at other times, the sea could sometimes be oily calm with, particularly between the Shetlands and Faeroes, countless basking sharks to be seen by day, or between Faeroes and Iceland a multitude of whales, sometimes spouts visible from horizon to horizon, all around. Yet this was only thirty years before the present depletion of the whale population by man. We were asked to count and record the whales as best we could when circumstances permitted; it was in any case necessary to distinguish between a whale and a U-boat schnorkelling, or at periscope depth. One of the Norwegian crews was once admiring a whale (one of the really big ones) when suddenly a Canadian Sunderland roared in across the field of view and laid a stick of depth charges across – but mercifully wide of – the line of the whale's progress.

On some flights we would go by way of the Faeroes, testing guns and bomb gear when clear of the land and any fishing vessels off the Shetlands and discouraging the fishing crew from shooting at the basking sharks. The landfall on the Faeroes would ensure an accuracy of the patrol. The incredible beauty of these islands was there, whether they were wreathed in cloud, or clear on a Sunday afternoon with many small boats fishing or sailing, or whether there was a full westerly gale blowing and beating against the western coasts of the islands. Once, we met a strange fishing vessel rather further out and went down to identify and photograph it. Just as we were coming in on the photographic run, it fired off two rockets with cables attached into our path. If it hoped to frighten us, it certainly did, but we were unscathed.

Leaving the Faeroes, we went out into the sea area between them and Iceland; the U-boat transit area, which their crews called the 'rosengarten', presumably because they would be harassed there (a garden full of thorns). Often at 1000 feet, we could see both the islands and Iceland at the same time, so great was the visibility in the clear polar air. At other times it would be so thick that visibility was less than a mile and you would imagine ships and submarines and so on in the murk and the rough seas. Although we used radar quite a lot, there were times when we had to observe radar silence, and, in any event, a good visual look-out by everyone was vital. It is extraordinary how habits persist, even now, over thirty years later in an aircraft, on a ship or looking out to sea, I scan the sea systematically as had become second nature on patrol.

Once, when dropping a flame float to take a measurement of drift, the object was immediately examined by a number of petrels, which flew in from apparently nowhere – although you could often see individual birds winging their way over the wave tops. Often the sea was fairly full of wreckage, particularly in the summer of 1944 north and east of Shetland, up to and beyond the Artic Circle; great oil slicks, aircraft wheels, wood and other objects and once the best part of a whole U-boat crew in their dinghies and life-jackets. On that day it was so calm and with little swell, that it was tempting to consider sending a message to request permission to land and capture them. But we were laden and in any case we heard on the radio that a naval ship was on its way to them; so we dropped a message to them, saying that a ship was on its way. A few hours later, on our way home, we intercepted the recall message to this vessel, due to approaching bad weather – it had not yet reached the U-boat crew and would not now do so.

This was the area where both Flying Officer Cruickshank (210 Squadron) and also Flight Lieutenant Hornell, RCAF (No. 162 Canso Squadron – Catalina amphibians) won their respective Victoria Crosses; in each case, their aircraft had been hit during the run-in to attack a U-boat. Jock Cruickshank, after depth charges failed to release on the first run, made a second attack, his navigator was killed and he received seventy-two wounds, but continued the attack and sank the U-boat. With the help of his second pilot, Sergeant Jack Garnett, who received a well-deserved DFM, he reached base, where the sinking aircraft was beached and where he was treated by our medical officer with a blood transfusion aboard the aircraft before being taken to the hospital near Lerwick. I shall return to this period later on.

Often, the patrols passed without any special incident except for the weather, the sighting of the regular neutral Swedish ship, or a strong contact on the radar which then disappeared. Now and again one saw a German aircraft and everyone always wanted to repeat the experience of Jack Fish, who had fought a Blohm and Voss 138 three-engined flying boat, a roughly equal match for a Catalina, for an hour before it made off towards its Norwegian base with one engine smoking. It was said that Jack was so exhausted from his efforts with the controls that he had to rest on a bunk for a while.

The patrol flown was usually a specific series of search

patterns, based on visibility distance (radar or visual) to cover a given area satisfactorily. Then that completed, one would set off to return to base. Occasionally a diversion signal would be received while out on patrol (due to weather or other reasons). The more usual diversions were to Reykjavik, Faeroes (Sorvagsvatn), Alness, Woodhaven on the Tay estuary (just below the bridge), or even Oban.

For a return to Sullom Voe, one would approach using the ASV (air-surface vessel radar) beacon set up on the hill behind the camp and for which we had a simple and satisfactory let down system which kept us clear of the 1450 foot high Ronas Hill at night and in bad weather. A night landing was quite frequent and this on a flying boat was a fascinating procedure, perhaps more for the pilots than for the crew in the cabin. As the final turn in was made, one set up a fixed rate of descent with power and airspeed by attitude. As the sea came nearer, the lights on the flare-path dinghies were still a little too far off to give any close approximation of height: This was given by the normal sensitive or the radar altimeter and one continued on the pre-set descent and seemed to be feeling downwards for the water with the part of one's anatomy enclosed within the proverbial seat of one's pants. The descent attitude was also a good one for touch-down, which sometimes would hardly be felt, at other times it was more definite and firm, power was taken off and the control column moved back, if the water was calm (the nose could dig in very strongly on calm water) or forwards, if there was any chop, to keep the hull on the water. Then there was the stall landing, normally done in daylight, but a bad night landing was some-times completed as a stall landing. This was a tail-down landing for use in very rough water, or on a swell. The engines had rather more power on than normal, slower speed and then at normal 'landplane' height for round out, power was taken off, the stick brought right back to stall the aircraft tail-first on to the water. The forward part of the hull fell forward onto the water, all the flying speed was lost and the aircraft remained down. The stall landing made an appalling noise for those inside the cabin, it sounded as though the floor was giving way. You pulled up literally in tens of yards.

Several times I had the pleasure of landing at the Faeroes on the lake of Vaagar Island, coming in between high cliffs, like pantomime scenery and over the top of the waterfall fed by the lake and which dropped down into the sea. To overshoot, or to take-off, under those usual wind conditions, one went in the same direction down the valley and over the little town. New Year's Eve, 1943, was spent with a Norwegian crew which had landed on Ronas Voe in Shetland due to poor weather. I was taken out to the anchored flying boat in the aircraft dinghy, we spent the night aboard and I flew the aircraft out to Sullom Voe the next morning, the weather having cleared.

Then to moorings; this process could take time and skill and luck. One never switched off the engines until the aircraft was safely on short slip, but there was a blipping switch to enable the engines to be used in the mooring approach. Drogues were also used to slow down the passage through the water towards the buoy and in a strong wind the aircraft could be 'sailed' with the aid of the big ailerons. Gear was then collected together; the moorings fully secured; covers put on the engines and we got aboard the dinghy to go ashore. With a feeling of great exhaustion we went up to the Operations Room for debriefing; a meal, bath and bed followed. But usually there was time for a drink or two before going to rest.

CHAPTER EIGHT

Spitsbergen and North Russia

In late August 1943, there was news of an impending operation in which we might be involved, but no details, so we just waited. Then one day in September, we had a very distinguished visitor in the person of Rev Tubby Clayton, founder of Toc H. Tubby was an army chaplain in WW1 and co-founded a non-denominational soldiers rest home at the front which became known as Toc H and is still doing good work today. He was clearly nothing to do with the expected task. He talked to people, looked at our camp and then expressed a wish to visit a broch – one of the ancient Shetland forts. My crew were nearly on the available list, but I was released to go with Tubby to see the broch. We went to one on the coast beyond Moss Bank. He talked interestingly about the site and then I noticed a car coming along the track. An airman came up and told me that I was to return with him at once to the camp. When I got back, I found considerable excitement, for it turned out that the expected operation was to have been in support of reconnaissance (by a joint Soviet/RAF Spitfire PR unit) of the *Tirpitz* and *Scharnhorst*, in Alten Fjord in North Norway. This was to lead to an attack on the ships. Unexpectedly, the ships had left the fjord they had rested in for so long and early that morning had attacked the small Norwegian garrison at Spitsbergen (Svalbard). Now we were to take-off as soon as possible and we did so at 1700 that day (8 September). But not before I had a telephone briefing with a naval officer at HQ No.18 Group (or the Admiralty) on the scrambler phone. I was told that we were to reconnoitre Ice Fjord and the settlements there, and then fly south on a given track to within a certain distance of the Norwegian coast, and then turn east and go into the Kola Inlet by Murmansk. If we found the *Tirpitz* and the *Scharnhorst* and their escort, we were to report their position, course and speed, shadowing them until, as the voice at the other end of the telephone said, "the home Fleet arrives, or you are shot down, or you reach PLE (prudent limit of endurance), when you are to go to Gryasnay in the Kola Inlet, land there and await further instructions."

There was then a cough at the far end of the line, "I have just been told that the Home Fleet has been ordered back to Iceland to refuel, so you must report and shadow the ships, if you find them, as long as you can, until you are shot down or reach PLE." So that was that.

Being early September, there was still virtually no real night the further north one flew in those latitudes. We took off with full tanks and no depth charges. Soon after take-off it became clear that the autopilot was serviceable (and shakily at that) on the rudder channel only. This was obviously going to be a great disadvantage, but no reason to return, when the important thing was to get on our way. We headed straight for the South Cape (Sorkapp) of Spitsbergen. Jacko was to be helped by Ross Bohm, our squadron navigation officer. We could see continuous low cloud or fog beneath us at sea level. We were not using radar at all. Early in the morning about 0200, after passing close to Bear Island, we saw, miles ahead, the peaks of Spitsbergen, near Sorkapp, pointing up through the cloud. The cloud over the sea began to clear as we got closer to the archipelago and we got down to sea level – a very calm and oily-like sea. We map-read up the coast towards the mouth of Ice Fjord and came round the corner, low over rocky shore, over a small lake, alarming a diver, and then we could see the smoke from the fires, but no sign of the warships which we had half-expected. First a quick look at Cape Linnhe wireless station, then to Barentburg and Green Harbour where the Soviet mining concession had been. All the buildings had been destroyed and fires were still burning. We took pictures, but could see no sign of any survivors. Then we flew along the coast towards Grumantby, the second mining settlement, it appeared to be hanging on the cliff face, there had been damage there also. Then on to the main Norwegian area at Longyearby, in Advent Bay. Here, there was the same scene of destruction and fire, on the rough airstrip which had been used by the Germans in 1942, there lay the wreckage of the Junkers Ju88 shot up and damaged by Tim Healey's aircraft a year before. In 1959 I was to walk and see it with my mother, aged seventy-six, and my daughter aged fourteen. We decided to examine all around Ice Fjord in case of a lurking destroyer or other vessel. We went around the fjord, with its great glaciers and with the remarkable mountains, there was no sign of the enemy, but plenty of the arctic beauty and the fantastic colours of the flowers on the moraines and the overall breathtaking Spitsbergen scene. One small isolated ice floe looked as if it was carrying a polar bear – but it was just the shape of part of the ice. We completed our reconnaissance. We heard later that one survivor who had fled into the hills, had seen us, hurried down to the shore but, not surprisingly, failed to attract our attention. Then we flew out of Ice Fjord and started our flight down the expected track of the German warships southwards. It had been assumed, rightly in fact, that they would steam back to Alten Fjord at all speed. Very soon we were noting signs of oil on the calm surface of the sea. Near Sorkapp, we suddenly saw a Ju88 flying towards and above us. This would be on its way to reconnoitre Ice Fjord, or on its way to supply by air, one of the remote German weather stations further north in the archipelago, which had been set up by U-boats, there was one in King's Bay. My first reaction was to be prepared for a possible attack, but there was convenient cloud nearby and we made for that. The Ju88 either did not see us, or was too busy to worry about a stray Catalina. The Catalina, with its powerful .5 inch guns in the blisters, was really very badly armed, for the field of fire was restricted by the tail and the wings and there were no auto-stops to the gun movement; all we had in the nose was the single .30 gun, which was no deterrent.

We broke out of the cloud and continued on and on over the still, glassy sea, with the sun gleaming, in and out of occasional sea fog, on manual control all the way, with just the little bit of aid from the rudder channel of the autopilot. The oil slicks seemed to get thicker, but still there was no sign of the German warships. We passed near Bear Island again, on and on, it was easy to get very drowsy in the bright sun, and yet one had to watch the height, keeping like a hawk and keep a lookout for any German aircraft. Then at last we reached the point about sixty miles off the Norwegian coast where we were to turn east. We did not see the coast as we were too low, but we had to be wary in case fighters were sent out. Finally, some hours later we turned south and made landfall east of the Kola Inlet, recognizing a village, Teriberka, on the coast east of Kildin Island. We let off the first of many colours of the day before we closed with the coast, we had come well supplied with these, for we knew that the Soviet forces would, although possibly expecting us, be very much on the alert. We turned round and made our way back to the mouth of the Inlet, with fairly frequent colours being fired. Twenty-two and three-quarters of an hour after take-off, we touched down on the Kola Inlet and taxyed towards the shore of the USSR; out came a motorboat crewed by Soviet girls. Skilfully, they took us in tow and we were brought to the shore, a wheeled beaching chassis was attached and we were up the slipway with efficiency in a very short time. Here, we were greeted by Soviet officers and officials, Admiral Archer, the British senior naval officer and the local RAF wing commander. We were very tired, but the main trouble seemed to be what to do about our homing pigeons. For as usual, we were carrying two homing pigeons in their yellow boxes, to release with a message, should we have to ditch. But first of all we were to have a meal and a very deep sleep. While we slept the pigeon problem was being debated at the appropriate level of Admiral, so well described by General Martel in his book on the work of the British Military Mission in the USSR. But he did not include or know of the final denouement.

The next day we were informed that we were allowed to exercise our pigeons in an enclosed space, inside an empty hospital ward. I took them along in their boxes and with a young Soviet nurse, by name, I believe, Rima, and some RN nursing orderlies, we let them go. The birds, relieved by being taken from the confinement of their boxes, expressed their relief to some effect, that would have delighted the most 'bowel-conscious' sister (I borrow the adjective from my professor of physiology of 1937!). The general hilarity was added to by the young nurse, whose English, at least in one question addressed to me, reflected the vocabulary of her Royal Naval (self-appointed) English tutor!

We had to await air reconnaissance confirmation of the return of the *Tirpitz* and *Scharnhorst* to their Alten Fjord base and, perhaps most important of all, an indication that they were returning to stay for some time. Their dispositions and boom defences had to be confirmed so that the midget submarines (X-craft), already at sea and en route with their parent submarines, could have the most up-to-date information for their attack. This was the operation that we were supporting. Our task was to fly the photo reconnaissance film back to England, for detailed interpretation there and the conversion of the information into target material for the X-craft crews.

Meanwhile, we spent our time in a visit to Murmansk. In spite of my lack of a valid licence, I drove the RAF lorry put at our disposal, as I did not trust any of the claims to driving prowess put forward by my crew! It was fascinating to see how a major overhaul of a Pe-2 was being done in the open by the roadside, out in the country, to avoid damage by German aircraft that might raid the aerodrome at Vaenga. Murmansk itself had been seriously damaged, but was still alive and operating; we spent a short time being entertained at the Intourist Club before returning.

On another day we were taken by launch to Admiral Archer's headquarters at Polyarnoye. We had distant views of Soviet submarines, on returning from patrol they would fire their guns to indicate the number of sinkings they had achieved, for they were busily engaged along the north Norwegian coast against supply vessels going to the Nazi garrisons. We heard much firing and also one morning during an alert, saw a German aircraft shot down in the distance over on the west side of the inlet.

The Northern Fleet Air Force at this time had some Bostons which they were using in the torpedo and anti shipping role. Their pilots' handling of these aircraft at low-level over the inlet was spectacular, expert and polished. Vaenga had earlier in the war been the base for the RAF Hurricane Wing, under a former Martlesham Heath test pilot, H. N. G. Ramsbotham-Isherwood, who was a wing commander at the time and was one of only four non-Russians to be awarded the Order of Lenin. Ramsbottom-Isherwood became CO of RAF Martlesham Heath. Sadly, he was killed in a Meteor flying accident in 1950. The Boston pilots had flown with the famous Twice Hero of the Soviet Union, Safronov, who had quickly become a highly skilled Hurricane pilot. Historically there was a lot to see, MBR-2 flying boats operated from Gryasnaya, but the real fascination was up at Vaenga where the operational aircraft also included the IL-2 and other aircraft. There was a 'graveyard' of aircraft, either damaged in raids, or which had been dumped as they became unserviceable. The guards did not seem unduly worried at our examining these fascinating aircraft – if only I had had my camera with me! There were I-15, I-16, I-153, SB-2, AR-2 and others. On at least one day a TB-3 landed at Vaenga, unfortunately I was not up at the airfield at the time. The 'graveyard' has often come back to my mind, what an opportunity for Soviet aircraft preservers, but this was

1943 and like us there was no time for Soviet airmen to think of preservation for posterity – they were too busy making history.

Squadron Leader F. A. Robinson commanded the RAF Spitfire (PRU) flight and they shared their work with the Soviet pilots. There was friendly and comradely rivalry in vying to get the best pictures, with the Soviet pilots getting some shots from extremely low-levels. Finally, the day came when the Spitfires had completed their sorties and it was felt that enough material was available and the situation stable enough, for the final briefing of the X-craft crews, with the big ships likely to stay in their present positions for some time. It was important that we wasted no time in getting our load back to England. The Soviet meteorological officers were worried about the weather for us, for there was a big gap between their area of information and the limits of that in England and we had to fly in that gap area. But we were prepared to go – we had aboard a full load of fuel – the Twin Wasps used 100 octane fuel, known colloquially between us and our Soviet hosts as 'bolshoi benzin'. They were at pains to show us samples; Mac looked at them and was satisfied. He also, typically, had made friends with the Soviet servicing staff and together with the aid of their equipment had made up a replacement plug for our APU.

Each of the Spitfire pilots had conducted eight to ten sorties over the Fjord under fire: Squadron Leader Robinson was to be awarded the Order of the Patriotic War (1st Class) for his work.

This first visit to the USSR had been fascinating for me and the seeds had been sown in my mind for learning more about the country and its language. A year later, with the possibility of a more regular convoy service I was asked to go as an RAF liaison officer at Murmansk – unfortunately this proposal fell through.

On the squadron we were always keen to fly on escort to Russian convoys and thus to help the Soviet war effort. There was no lack of volunteers for the special flights either. There were then, and even now, signs that the work, the sacrifice of sailors, both Royal and Merchant Navy, the whole contribution were much appreciated, but it rankles when it is minimized in some official Soviet histories. Little did the post-war Soviet Government under Stalin realize, with its harder line view and its attitude, how much goodwill for their country was lost. But even that shortsightedness can never dampen my admiration for the tremendous sacrifices made by the Soviet people for our joint cause.

We had a discussion with Admiral Archer and Squadron Leader Robinson, who could give advice about the local meteorological situation and what it might signify further west, together with the Soviet meteorological officers and the interpreter. I was quite determined to go; we could ride through whatever might be in the way. So at last light (or what went for last light at that time of year) on 15 September, we taxyed out into the Kola Inlet and took off. Already, after a week it was noticeably darker and as we went out to sea, then parallel to the northern coast of Norway, it was quite dark. Cloud increased above and below and as we turned onto a south-south-west course out to sea and parallel to the main line of the west Norwegian coast, the wind appeared to be increasing. But we were not to realize by how much until the next morning, when we let down to the west to come out over the sea. Ten minutes later we sighted one of the neutral Swedish ships on its track and we calculated that during the night, we must have drifted over Norway. The sea state and a drift observation showed just how strong the wind had been and so I did a quick check bearing on the DF set. We were to fly past Shetland, past Invergordon and go into Woodhaven on the Tay Estuary, where it was fairly calm, but a stall landing was necessary. We touched down at Woodhaven twenty and a quarter hours out from Grasnaya – and we had flown direct, not via Spitsbergen! We hurried with our load of film up the road to Leuchars, where we were to rest and a Mosquito was standing by to take our films to, presumably, Benson. We were told later that this first Mosquito had to return because of engine trouble, but the reserve aircraft got away, the film was interpreted and the information was sent to the X-craft midget submarines. A few days later we were to be thanked by Admiralty signal for our part in 'Operation Source'. Mac was later to be one of the aircrews to receive a Soviet award – the Medal for Valour (Medal' za otvagu).

The X-craft submarines attacked on 22 September 1943 and damage to the *Tirpitz* kept it out of service for at least six months. Many of the crews were killed and several received decorations including two being awarded Victoria Crosses (VCs).

CHAPTER NINE

Winter 1943 – 1944

After the return from Spitsbergen and Murmansk, we began to settle down for the winter and started preparations for operating with the Leigh Light on the new Catalina IV aircraft which we were expecting. The Leigh Light was the searchlight for illuminating the submarine on the surface at night, so that a satisfactory attack could be made. On the Catalina the light was mounted under the starboard wing, extra batteries had to be carried and the result was a discouraging addition to the weight and drag of the aircraft. Previously, we had a procedure using flares, which, although extremely hit and miss, was at least without detriment to the performance of the aircraft. Furthermore, if an engine failure was experienced, there was grave doubt if the Catalina would still have its good single-engined performance. So we were not enthusiastic about the light, but rumours of a new radar to replace the old faithful and operationally effective Mark II ASV, were much more welcome. At the same time, we were training on the new Mark III Low-Level Bombsight. This was an extremely accurate device, but involved the navigator aiming and releasing the bombs, or depth charges in our case. To take this task from the pilot, who had to do the aiming and dropping of the depth charges by eye and skill, was as bad as computerizing cricket. Now, instead of the pilots showing their skill in aiming practice bombs against the target towed across the waters of the Voe by a pinnace, the pilots were relegated to the bus driver role, while the navigators produced excellent and constant results. It mattered little that this was what was done in Bomber Command.

The patrols flown that winter included one air-sea rescue alert, which came to nothing. Then returning from another patrol north of the Faeroes ('Hancox'), which was an area from which we hoped for some new success, my crew and I were one night forced up rather higher than usual, though not as high as Squadron Leader Stuart Hall used to go; thereby irritating and freezing his crew! We ran into sudden and heavy icing in a clear space between two cloud layers with rain (supercooled) falling from the top layer, this was actually freezing rain which is extremely dangerous even with de-icing. Our de-icers were already operating, but just could not cope with the sudden accretion. The Catalina smartly lost speed and began to drop rapidly. We were just a few miles north of the Faeroes; they were visible on the radar at just over five miles. In spite of full power, the aircraft continued to drop and drop, at 4000 ft, with the higher parts of the islands not far ahead and not far below, there was nothing to do but to jettison the depth charges! We sent them down 'safe'. The blunt stores must have made a terrifying noise as they fell down through the darkness towards the islands. As far as I know, they fell in the sea. This lightened us, so we could at least fly level. Gradually, we got the aircraft to climb into a warmer layer of air where we lost the ice and things became normal, except that we could not go into Sullom Voe, we were diverted to Alness.

We stayed a few days at Alness, which gave us an opportunity to see old friends and also my relations at Contin near Dingwall. Our next operation was to be from Sullom Voe and so we flew a transit flight back there, with a few passengers on their way to Sullom.

These winter flights were brightened by displays of the Northern Lights, and even occasionally, the rare spectacle of a moon-caused rainbow. While flying by day low over a cloud bank, the aircraft's shadow formed a 'broken spectre' effect, such as had been very common off Gibraltar, the year before.

I referred in the last chapter to the carriage of pigeons, we had an airman in charge of these at Sullom Voe and one day orders came that the birds were no longer to be carried and were to be returned to the mainland. This was one of those rather inexplicable and unnecessary decisions that can so easily affect morale; even if we had been told that we were going to carry dinghy radios. The decision was challenged and within forty-eight hours weight was added to the plea, as one of our Catalinas returning in bad weather disappeared on the approach and nothing was heard of it. In fact it had landed in the sea near Papa Stour, one of the outer Shetland Islands in a smooth area of water, but very remote. It was only located, because within an hour or so, one of the pigeons came in giving the position. Even if the pigeon had come in without a message, a search area of probability could have been worked out. But on the ground things had moved fast and I had set off with a team of volunteers, including Norwegians, to climb Ronas Hill in case, as we feared, the aircraft had flown into the hill's north-west face. My fell walking in the Lake District before the war and the Ben Wyvis climb helped, for we were on compass and map-read after going into thick cloud at about 100 feet above sea level. The walk was heavy going as we hurried to the top and searched the faces, but we found nothing and got the good news of the crew's location and subsequent rescue when we got back. But all this nothwithstanding, the pigeons were sent off on the next ship or aircraft to the mainland. The airman was very upset and had to be put on duties which were obviously not to his liking. But the story has a happy ending, within a week all the pigeons reportedly flew back to their loft at Sullom and the airman was reinstated. We continued to carry the birds and what the Air Ministry thought we did, or if they even knew, did not matter! A little before this time we had received the first of the dinghy radios whose aerial had to be launched by a kite, initially propelled into the air by a sort of rocket device. Flight Lieutenant West, our gunnery leader, gave a memorable demonstration of the device. His first shot went rather horizontally across the calm waters of the Voe, mercifully missing aircraft at moorings, and disappeared into the cabin of a works lorry, where the driver was peacefully eating his sandwiches! He leapt from the cab to protest in no uncertain terms about the sudden and fiery interruption of his lunch hour. It was no wonder we preferred the greater reliability of the pigeons.

On another occasion we took some of the pigeons out for their regular training exercise. We took them out to Esha Ness. After releasing them, we explored the cliffs, including the magnificent Houlls of Scraada (Holes of the Devil). If you imagine an inlet from the sea which comes some thirty yards or more into the cliff and enters a cave; inland perhaps as far as 150 yards from the cliff edge; a stream flows into a large hole in the ground, perhaps fifty feet deep with a waterfall – that would come close. Erosion has connected this hole with the inlet and the hole is in fact a beach, connected to the sea by a subterranean tunnel. As the Atlantic swell rolls in and blows up the tunnel, so it sends up a great cloud of water and spray from the inland hole. One day, of course, the tunnel will fall in and the whole thing will become a deep inlet into the cliff, but meanwhile it is a wonderful and awe-inspiring sight when a really heavy sea is running to give the full effect, both visual and sound, as the water rises from the greensward. Excellent mushrooms grow on this turfed headland.

There were other outings during the autumn and winter; walks to Moss Bank, where there was the little pier for the overland route to Yell (bus and boat from Lerwick up to Unst), as opposed to the calling steamer from Lerwick to Balta Sound in Unst. Round here one would often see Arctic Skuas. On the hillside above was the little farm, known as 'Moss Bank Kate's', where you could get an excellent high tea of bacon and eggs, or haddock and eggs (and there was sometimes a dram of whisky for the favoured). We went hare shooting (without success), the Shetland hares would turn white in winter, regardless of the fact that although there was snow, it was not often very thick on the ground. There was sea fishing (mainly in the summer) and

1   Supermarine Stranraer Mk1 K7290 at Felixstowe. This aircraft later served with 240 Squadron and sank on the 21 November 1940 at Stranraer. Pictured from the author's boat

2   MAEE Felixstowe in the mid 1930s from the author's boat

3   HP42 Heracles in the winter's slush in 1934

4   Hendon Air Display 1936

5   Spitfire prototype K5054 at Hendon Air Display 1936, New Types Park

6   Hawker Hart at University of
London Air Squadron (ULAS)
summer camp

7   Early Hurricane Mk1 of 111 Squadron photographed at RAF Northolt in 1938

8   Aerial View of RAF Upavon 1939

9   The wreckage from the Heinkel He11 bomber rammed by Sgt Hancock over RAF
Windrush 18 August 1940

10   Wreckage of Hancock's Anson

11   Sally and John French in Great Rissington 1940

12   The bomb damage at RAF Brize Norton on 16 August 1940 that destroyed over forty aircraft

13 John French in Link Trainer

14 Airspeed Oxford in a winter scene

15   Catalina on patrol

16   Catalina releasing a depth charge

17 U601 after being attacked by the author's aircraft

18 U601 sinking after the attack

R.A.F. Form 96.		MESSAGE FORM.		Office Serial No.	
S 575 (Naval)				No. of Groups	Office Date Stamp.
Call IN				GR	
and —					
Preface OUT					

(Above this line is for Signals use only)

TO*

210 SQUADRON (R) SULLOM VOE

FROM* A.O.C. 18 GROUP   Originator's Number ... 4 ... /   Date ....   Your/my

MY CONGRATULATIONS TO S/LDR. FRENCH AND HIS CREW ON TODAY'S SPLENDID AND

SUCCESSFUL ATTACK ON A U-BOAT. MY CONGRATULATIONS ALSO TO THE MAINTENANCE PERSONNEL

CONCERNED WHOSE EFFICIENT MAINTENANCE OF THE AIRCRAFT AND ALL ITS COMPLICATED

EQUIPMENT ENABLED THE AIRCREW TO MAKE THIS SUCCESSFUL ATTACK AND BRING BACK

PHOTOGRAPHIC EVIDENCE OF THE KILL.

This message must be sent AS WRITTEN and may .... be sent by W/T. Signature	This message must be sent IN CYPHER and may .... be sent by W/T. Signature	Originator's Instructions.* Degree of Priority.*	Time of Origin. ▪1835A
			T.O.R.
‡ Originator to insert "NOT" if message is not to go by W/T over any part of the route.		(Below this line is for Signals use only.)	T.H.I.

System in	Time in	Reader	Sender	System out	Time out	Reader	Sender	System out	Time out	Reader	Sender

19   Signal about U-boat U601 sinking

240 TAIN. 20-7-44/IC/120 F63 - 3 DINGHIES WITH SURVIVORS 68°37'N 09°25'E. - 150'

20   Liberator Crew awaiting rescue

Air Force Cross

London Gazette dated 1.9.44.

S/L. Frank John FRENCH D.F.C. (72120) No.210 Sqdn.

This officer was captain of a Catalina whose crew
volunteered on 21st July, 1944, to take part in the rescue
of 6 survivors of a Liberator which had been shot down into
the sea 2 days previously. The sortie necessitated landing
in the open sea 540 miles north of the Shetlands. The
survivors were located and, 45 minutes later, S/L. French
took off, rescuing all six men. This difficult feat was
accomplished without damage to his aircraft. This
officer's shrewd judgment, skill and experience of seamanship,
together with his practical first aid arrangements on the
homeward journey, undoubtedly saved the lives of the aircrew members.

21 Citation about Liberator rescue

22 Bee (John French's wife) and
a souvenir German incendiary
bomb!

23   Catalina at Spitsbergen

24   Bee and Valerie (John's
daughter and the editor's Mum!)
with Mosquito in 1947

FEBRUARY	12	CATALINA IV	JX222 W	SELF	CREW + F/O WICKSON SGT OSBORNE. P/O O'TOOLE S/LT THOMAS CREW.	A/S PATROL . S.W. FAEROES.
	17	,,	JX246 R	,,	CREW. P/S STEWART	TEST. BOMBING & GUNNERY
	25	,,	JX223 M	,,	F/O SCHMUCK. ,, JACKSON. FARMER. P/O McGUINTY.+ F/S DAWSON.	A/S ESCORT — NOT MET . 517 kts. U-BOAT ATTACKED WITH 2 D.C. SURVIVORS SEEN IN WATER; U-BOAT
,,	,,	,,			W/O HAMMETT. SGT TONER. SGT BROWN	SANK STERN FIRST. 70°26'N 12°4'E DESTRUCTION CONFIRMED . 29.ii.44

+ Soviet Medal of Valour 1944 ‖ This U-boat was U601, a 517t.
VII C boat. 773 tons surf. 882 sdn.
Diesels 2 1400 H.P. 215-220
37mm. 2 M.G. 2 Sng tried 500 H.P. LENGTH

SUMMARY FOR : FEBRUARY 1944.	CATALINA IV. OPS
No: 210 Squadron.	Non Ops
29. ii. 44.	33-25 —
𝓕.𝓙. French S/L for F/Cmdr.	—

ARCH — — - NO FLYING F.J. French S/L.

25   Excerpt from J French Log book covering sinking of UBoat

---

SUMMARY FOR JUNE 1944	CATALINA
UNIT : 210 Squadron.	
DATE: 1.vii.44. 62.15	PASSENGER
F.J. French S/L	

JULY	1	CATALINA.	JX257 Q	SELF	CREW+P/O RANGE	A/S PATROL. U/B Survivors ·Hit flares sighted, Mustn (aircraft wheeled)
-	9	—	JX202 O	,,	,, + W/C ISACKE	,, ; landed Oban
,,	11	,,	JX202 O	—	,, + F/S GROSSO S/L SPENCE	OBAN — Loch Ness — SULLOM Mine.
,,	17	,,	JX202 O	,,	F/L WRAIGHT	A/S PATROL . N.W. Lofoten .
,,	21	,,	JX299 X	,,	CREW M.B.E. F/O Somerville	Air Sea Rescue of Liberator crew (F/86) in dinghies 62 hrs
,,	,,	,,		(S/L Nelms D.F.C.	W/O Contant	(F/86) 68° 40'N 09°55'E. Ocean
,,	,,	,,		F/L Grey	Sgt Toner & 3 members lost.	landing & take off! A.O.C. signal
,,	,,	,,		Sgt Gregory		
-	-	,,	— K	—	CREW + F/S SMART.	—
,,	26	,,	JX262	SELF		A/S PATROL diverted Reykjavik.
,,	28	,,	JX261	,,	— ,, —	A/S Transit Reconnaissance. Reykjavik — Shetlands — Alness
-	-	,,	,,	,,	,, ,,	
,,	30	,,	JX262	—	F/S SHEPHERD	ALNESS — SULLOM VOE.

GRAND TOTAL [Cols. (1) to (10)]
2145 Hrs. 00 Mins.   TOTALS CARRIED FORWARD

26   Excerpt from J French Log book covering rescue of Liberator crew

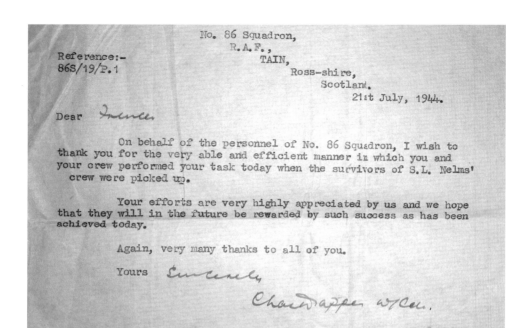

No. 86 Squadron,
R.A.F.,
TAIN,
Ross-shire,
Scotland.
21st July, 1944.

Reference:-
86S/19/P.1

Dear *French*,

On behalf of the personnel of No. 86 Squadron, I wish to thank you for the very able and efficient manner in which you and your crew performed your task today when the survivors of S.L. Nelms' crew were picked up.

Your efforts are very highly appreciated by us and we hope that they will in the future be rewarded by such success as has been achieved today.

Again, very many thanks to all of you.

Yours *Sincerely*

Chadwick W/Cdr.

S.L. French, D.F.C.,
No. 210 Squadron,
R. A. F.

27 Letter from Liberator crew's Officer Commanding

28 Catalina flying back from Spitsbergen

29 The start of another long patrol

Mr. Kruschev (second from right) and Marshal Bulganin on their visit to
R.A.F. Marham in April, 1956.

30 Khrushchev's visit to the UK in 1956 with the Author

31 Wing Commander John French's medals. The small case includes his watch – this was almost lost when he was wiping the outside of the screen and the strap came undone – the only thing that stopped it going overboard was a wrist hair! Also in the case is his lucky cat and parts of the Oxford aircraft that crashed near Bibury.

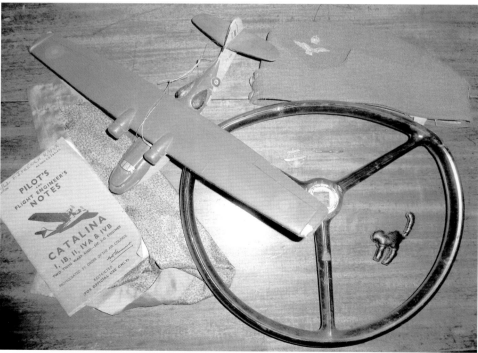

32 The silk flying scarf (worn during long Catalina patrols), a recognition model painted as his aircraft, a Catalina control yoke and his Catalina Pilot's Notes. John French was an avid collector of souvenirs! Also shown, is a side cap and two trench art badges – a U Boat with the letter F (for his nickname 'Froggie') and a catalina.

brown and sea trout fishing. The latter used to be caught at the mouth of the stream, near the airfield at Scatsta. I often wonder what has happened to all that area which the camp did not really spoil, now that the oil terminal work has begun. Has the little house that formed the front of the mess vanished? Have our huts, hangars and the ground crew huts, where they proudly chalked up on the walls the record of their aircraft and crews' exploits gone forever?

We bought Shetland shawls and Fair Isle (Shetland) pattern knitwear. These were often knitted by the women as they walked along tending the sheep, with the traditional patterns, hearts, diamonds and so on being incorporated. We would sometimes go down to the hotel in Lerwick for a change of scene. But our main recreation was at the camp, the cinema, the occasional ENSA (Every Night Something Awful) show. We had Gracie Fields once, Bernard Miles and John Mills another time; then each mess had its night with the station dance band in attendance. The Officers' Mess night was Saturday. The mess had been built to replace part of the old '*Manila*', the ship moored in the Voe, like the '*Batavia*' at Invergordon. These ships had now gone on elsewhere. We had a big anteroom in the mess and here the band would play. Professional musicians all, they were an essential part of the life of the whole camp. They played popular tunes, RAF songs, our own local RAF songs, such as 'One day I know I'll go far away from Sullom Voe . . .' and 'They sent us off to Norway at two hundred . . . feet.' This last was said to have been originated by the Norwegian 333, but I think it probably dates from 1940 and the early recces over Norway by Hudsons and Beauforts, only later getting its chorus of 'We were flying Catalina, (thrice) . . .' We also had the occasional dance in the Mess.

Then, on the nights that the band was at the NAAFI or at the Sergeants' Mess, there were our own entertainments. One of our controllers had a magnificent repertoire of RAF songs and accompanied himself on the piano. He had them written down in notebooks, words and all. One awful day, he was found to be burning these priceless books and none were recovered. Then later in 1944, when he returned from his captain's course, we had Graham Dowson with his Gibraltar take-off act; various imitations, including Winston Churchill, and other acts. At the bar there were so many good friends one can remember – Bunny Austin, our Marine Craft officer; the controllers, Skerret-Rogers, Whisky Walker (indeed of the firm of Johnny Walker and who provided whisky for the Mess, but not to be confused with the pilot of the same nickname) and Spence (Royal Aero Club secretary in peacetime, ex-World War I, who came flying with us to see what he was controlling from his desk); John Browning, our Intelligence Officer; Angus Campbell and his RAF assistant and Robbie, our Norwegian Intelligence Officer. We shared all this Mess with No.330 Norwegian Squadron (and with No.333 when they sent their detachments). No.330 had Sunderlands and were commanded by Commander Thorsten Diesen. He once had a Canadian Sunderland crew attached to his squadron and they had an unlucky taxying accident in the Voe. Thorsten went aboard to give them the expected rocket. He went out in a dinghy, which then waited by the door of the Sunderland. Just as he was about to return to the dinghy, Thorsten remembered something else which he wished to add, he turned back facing into the aircraft, made his remarks and then stepped back into the dinghy which wasn't there, straight into the February waters of the Voe. Unfortunately, the dinghy had made off to some emergency in the course of his last remarks, not warning the unfortunate Thorsten. It required several rums to stop the cold and restore some composure to our good friend Thorsten. His flight commanders were Per Thorendahl and R. Kaldager. Among the pilots were Thurmann-Neilsen (who also occasionally flew the Northrop seaplane) and many others with whom we worked together in a happy family crowd. There were frequent visits from Woodhaven, near Leuchars, where the remarkable No.333 (Norwegian) Squadron with Catalina, the slowest, and Mosquito, one of the fastest operational aircraft were based. The Mosquito part of the squadron was based at Leuchars. Their CO was that fine pilot Commander Jergensen (later to be Air Attache in London). He was at home on either type of aircraft. He was to be killed in an accident involving an American F-100 when I was in Norway in 1959 and it was a sad day to have to attend his funeral, but I was proud to be there as representative of those days in Shetland. The 333 pilots on Catalinas included Lieutenants Kraft, Vik and others. Down at Scalloway, were the Norwegian motor torpedo boats (MTBs), which, apart from their operations about which we learnt little, provided us with Norwegian Christmas trees – collected while they operated clandestinely in Norway. (Scalloway was for a time the headquarters of The Shetland Bus – Norwegian Resistance)

Around Christmas 1943, the *Scharnhorst* took to sea against a Russian-bound convoy, the *Tirpitz* had been too badly damaged by the midget submarine and other attacks to put to sea. My crew was at standby for a long-range reconnaissance, the weather was vile and it was an alarming thought to have to fly up to the distant Arctic waters, but we were ready to go and would have gone gladly. However, as is well known, the Royal Navy found the *Scharnhorst* and finished its career.

Early in 1944 we became No.210 Squadron instead of No.190, Wing Commander Pat Alington was posted back to No.18 Group and Wing Commander Lawrence Burgess took his place. Stuart Hall (for a short time he had been Chief Navigation Instructor at Invergordon), F. W. Thomas and I, were the flight commanders, though I was given the title of Squadron Leader Training.

The Shetlands, for all the words of the song which we sang about leaving 'these . . . Shetlands far behind', was a wonderful spot to work and live in. Cut off in our outpost, we were very happy and felt that we were doing a useful job, even if for a time, U-boat sightings had become very few and far between. But this was the lull before 1944. We had high morale and we knew it, and we knew we were happy. Our mail – letters from our families and for me from friends at old South Cerney and other friends, used to come in regularly by the civil airline via Sumburgh, or the occasional 'Sparrow' – the passenger version of the old pre-war Harrow bomber – into Scatsta. This also – as did the old LNER '*Vienna*' and other troopships – brought us reinforcements and took away the time expired. We were visited by VIPs including Sir Archibald Sinclair, Secretary of State for Air and by the Inspector-General.

We played squash and golf. There was one hole on the course which could easily be done in one, if the ball was bounced accurately on the Marine Craft Section hut (where the off duty watch was asleep) and went straight into the hole. Success was not recorded by drinks all round, but by the chorus of protest from within the hut. We had fine hot baths in the peat-stained water in the bathhouse, followed by an almost Russian like rush from the bathhouse to ones' quarters in the nearby wooden hut, through the winter's icy air. There, snow sometimes came through the cracks under the door, while the red-hot 'Rosa' stoves roared and cast sparks from their chimneys. We would cook omelettes and cocoa, before going to bed.

I was on holiday a year or so after the war, with my wife and Aberdeen Terrier (*Sally*), in Shetland and we went to Sullom Voe. An unhappy party of care and maintenance officers were in the Mess and told us they found it all very boring. They received us hospitably, but I was saddened. There were too many ghosts, many of them happy people, no longer with us, and I think these ghosts were saddened too. Even without the stimulus of war, how could one be bored in Shetland?

One other activity a little later on in 1944 was when the '*Maid of Thule*' visited the Voe to inspect our moorings. Among the crew of this former fishing vessel was Johnny Robertson, the veteran Shetland diver who had worked on the scuttled German Fleet after the first war in Scapa Flow. As a result of a rashly expressed wish at the bar before lunch, which I have never regretted, I found myself an hour later being dressed in the full panoply of a diving suit and helmet, with traditional red knitted cap to assuage the draught from the air being pumped down to the helmet, on the deck of the 'Maid'. I was put over the side and, although a virtual non-swimmer all my life, found nothing to fear, only the complete fascination of looking up at the bottom of the 'Maid of Thule' and then at the sea bed of the Voe in the cold water of a Shetland February afternoon. There was not a lot to see, crabs scurrying away and one fish, it was a bit murky, with the water not too clear.

Cecil White, always game to try anything unusual, had joined me in this outing, but oddly enough for his build, his wrists were rather small and when he went down after me, the water leaked in past the rubber wrist grips and down his sleeves into the suit. He pulled on the recall rope and was pulled up , got aboard, sat down and undressed in the customary manner – for with the heavy equipment and the leads, the diver out of water is pretty helpless. His trousers were wet and, although this was clearly due to the leak at the wrists, the resultant back chat and comments were unmerciful, "Mr White, it can't have been as frightening as that!" was the least. We repeated this outing the next time the 'Maid of Thule' came into the Voe and John Browning joined us. On this occasion the vessel was anchored on the edge of a shallow area, with deeper water nearby. Although I went down fifteen feet or more, when John went down, with his glasses on, he suddenly set off at quite high speed and in the wrong direction. Eventually, he broke surface with his helmet out of the water (but still fairly buoyant) about up to his neck, he walked about in this sort of 'periscope depth' situation and then finally went back into deeper water. His glasses had misted up and he was quite unaware that this remarkable scene had taken place; he was sure that he had been submerged the whole time and could not understand our laughter.

Once or twice we were given warning of the approach of enemy aircraft from the direction of Lerwick, but nothing came of these, although Sullom had been a target earlier in the war. One unlucky Ju88 surprised a gun position at Lerwick in 1943 or 1944 and the soldiers loosed off a shot to warn the next position along the coast. It was a lucky shot, for it hit and shot off the 88's tail. While I was at Sullom we were visited by one high-flying reconnaissance aircraft. I observed this sound from the safety of the lavatory, a similar situation to that of Jack Bellingham in the (1940) Brize Norton attack!

There were always quite a few rumours around. One resulted in a search of the area by all available crews after a report that a U-boat had been seen to put men ashore in a lonely firth and had taken some sheep. The party arrived too late to intercept the raiders. Eventually it was admitted by the Navy in Lerwick, that it had been one of our own submarines, setting off on patrol of Norwegian waters, whose crew had felt that their fresh meat supplies were a little meagre and had decided to augment them.

CHAPTER TEN

Operations in 1944

As February 1944 came towards its end, the crew and I were detailed to escort Russian convoy JW 57, to be met far away, north of the Arctic Circle. We were to take-off fairly late that day. In the afternoon, while walking along the shore of the Voe I saw twenty-five migrating herons (my 'lucky' bird) on the shore not far from the camp. The flight was to be long, there was little daylight up north at that time of the year and the weather picture showed that we would be flying against strong northerly winds, with front after front and snow storms and icing. The air would be bumpy and altogether it was not one of the most promising situations. We were loaded with full overload tanks and only a pair of depth charges. Our scheduled time with the convoy was to be rather less than two hours, as I remember. We used the radar sparingly as we neared the convoy, but had been told that one of the ships was carrying a radar responder beacon on to which we might home. Suddenly, when not far off our ETA (estimated time of arrival), we got a return on the radar. We let down out of the cloud to see beneath us a rough sea, an angry, ugly sea, with snow flurries all around and then, some miles off, the wake of a ship. I suddenly realized that this was not a surface ship of the convoy escort, but a submarine. As we dived and accelerated towards the vessel, Jacko made a quick check that there were no Royal Naval submarines in the area. As we came closer the U-boat opened fire with 37mm and machine gun fire, the tracers coming lazily and then faster towards us and the shells exploding. The fire was erratic because of the heavy sea and the U-boat Captain unwisely decided to remain on the surface. Our own nose gunner fired a few shots with the .30 gun, but that soon packed up with a stoppage. We got down to attack level and approached up the line of the stern, the firing had, I think stopped. I pressed the release button and away went our two depth charges; we were at a pretty low height. We turned to see the result. Bill McGuinty had opened the blister and had been hard at work with the K.20 camera. It was said that he was halfway out of the blister with Jock Brown holding on to his feet. His pictures were perfect and within a few days it was confirmed that the U-boat (later to be identified as U-601) had been definitely sunk. Visually, as we turned, we saw the bows rise as the U-boat came out from between the subsiding plumes of the explosions and by the time we got round and passed over the scene, only a few men, some odd bits of wreckage and patches of oil were in the water. One man shook his fist at us. Next time round there was only wreckage, no sign of life, except for the seabirds wheeling over the scene. Then the snow flurries closed in, blocking the scene, the sea marker and position 70° 26' N, 12° 40' E from sight, but never from memory. We failed to find the convoy or its escorts and our time being more or less up, our depth charges used, we set off back to Shetland, making excellent time with the strong tailwind, but failing to get our attack message through because of the bad radio conditions, until half an hour or so from the base. Presumably, our signal was intercepted by the convoy, but it would not have relayed it. One mystery was the radar return that we had picked up – with coding – perhaps it was a reflected signal or perhaps it was some German device to confuse.

Reading an account in Russian about the operations of the Soviet Northern Fleet, I was interested to see several references to U-601, which seems to have given much trouble to the Soviet forces in the war, earlier on in the Novaya Zemlya area. She had once destroyed a Soviet Catalina at anchor in the bay – and it was Catalina M/210 which had destroyed her.

So 1944 had started in good style and soon 330 Squadron were to get a sighting. Then there was a lull until May, when the patrols were moved towards the Norwegian coast and later much further north. Before this we were to lose an aircraft, which, while on an air test, crashed through low cloud into a hill overlooking the Voe. It was an accident which occurred just as the Wing Commander was remarking at a conference of pilots, "We have been lucky with accidents". All at once there was a loud explosion about half a mile away and through the window flames and smoke could be seen rising up. I ran off to the scene, which took a little time across the boggy ground and found that all the occupants were dead in the wreckage. Owing to the fire and exploding ammunition it was impossible to remain within the wreckage to check how many people had been on board, but it seemed that there were less than I feared. A number of our navigators had been aboard to swing the compasses and the loop aerial on the water before the air test. But finding that they had not got any extra Mae Wests aboard, they decided – they could not easily explain why – to go ashore, rather than take a chance. Whatever the reason for this prudence, they were fortunate. Among them was Jacko. The aircraft seemed to have hit the hill at a fairly low forward speed, but at a fair rate of descent, breaking it up on impact. Perhaps it was stalled, when the ground was suddenly seen through the breaking clouds. This aircraft was JX210, which crashed on Garth Hill on the 25 March 1944, with the loss of seven lives.

With patrols off the Norwegian coast, both sightings and sinkings began. These started off with an attack by Lieutenant Thurmann Neilsen of No.330 Norwegian Squadron. He was successful in sinking a U-boat, but the aircraft was badly damaged by gunfire; the starboard outer engine stopped and the inner was severely damaged. However, this skilful and much respected pilot got his aircraft and crew safely back to base.

Between 16 and 30 May, twenty-two sightings resulted in thirteen attacks and six sinkings. One of these was the work of Jacko, Flying Officer Jackson RCAF, my navigator, flying (while I was away) as navigator to a South African Air Force crew under Captain Maxwell. Jacko was using the Mark III bombsight on which he had put much practice and he was awarded the DFC for his part in the attack. Another U-boat was sunk by Flying Officer Bastable, also of 210 Squadron. It was in this 'Northern Transit' area that the Canso (Catalina) amphibians of No.162 (Canadian) RCAF Squadron had their triumphs and losses, Flight Lieutenant D. E. Hornell earning his posthumous Victoria Cross after sinking a U-boat, which also shot his aircraft into the sea. Lieutenant Kraft of 333 Squadron flying from Sullom Voe also sank a U-boat.

On D-Day, Mac, Jacko and I were aboard the aircraft carrier HMS *Victorious* cruising on a diversionary sortie off the Norwegian coast. We joined her at Scapa, having flown down from Shetland in a Catalina with Jimmy Mountford, who then flew back. After being entertained on board HMS *Duke of York* by the Commander-in-Chief Home Fleet and I had been pecked by the famous tame Golden Eagle, Mr Ramshaw (owned by Captain Knight, another guest on board the flagship), we transferred to *Victorious*. My father served on an earlier *Victorious* many years before. Nothing occurred during our sortie and on its completion we were flown off the flight deck in Barracudas and on from Orkney in a Sea Otter to Scatsta. Oddly enough, while I was on this expedition, my brother, who was in the Navy, was sampling flying in a Catalina from Gibraltar, as a change from his navigational duties on the carrier, HMS *Stalker*.

In July the patrol area was moved up north, to the west of the Lofoten Islands. The operation was further aided by our squadron, as most aircraft now had the new Mark VIII radar, which operated on a higher frequency and shorter wave length than our old Mark II. In seven days there were fifteen attacks, three U-boats being sunk and three seriously damaged. But generally, the seas were very calm and the U-boats were well able to stay on the surface with a steady gun platform and fight back at the attacking aircraft. It was in such a situation that Flying Officer J. Cruickshank of our squadron won his Victoria Cross on 17 July.

On 18 July, a Liberator of No.86 Squadron (F/86, captained by Squadron Leader Nelms) was set on fire during an attack on a U-Boat and was forced to ditch, some 100 miles west of the Lofoten Islands. One of the crew was killed in the ditching, but the other eight members of the crew took to dinghies. Two however, drifted away from the others and were not seen again. The six survivors were then in three K-type single seater dinghies. On 19 July a Catalina (K/210) went out, but failed to find the crew; but on 20 July they were re-sighted, in a different area, and the sea state was reported favourable for landing. On 20 July I was sitting with Group Captain G. F. Humphries, our Station Commander, in his office and he had just said, "We are now going to draft a citation for the award of the Victoria Cross to Flying Officer Cruickshank," when the telephone rang and the news about the Liberator crew's position came in. I was called away to get ready to go out in search of the lost crew and to try and pick them up. I was briefed over the telephone by AOC No.18 Group (Air Vice-Marshal Simpson). He told me that I was to locate and pick up the crew, if possible, but on no account to hazard my aircraft or to risk its loss.

We got together a volunteer crew of seven, our Medical Officer, Squadron Leader O'Connor, badly wanted to come too, but space was going to be at a premium and we wanted a lightened aircraft in the event of landing and for the subsequent take-off. We re-fuelled to 1200 gallons and took off at 0130 on the morning of 21 July. As we flew northwards, I went over the landing and take-off tactics over and over again in my mind, perhaps several hundred times. Half an hour before our ETA at the reported position I took some anti seasickness pills (and more later on the water); there would be no point in getting seasick before the take-off, if we picked the crew up. Jacko's navigation was excellent and we sighted the crew in their dinghies almost on ETA. At the same moment they sent up flares. The position was 68° 40' N, 09° 53' E. We reported that we had found them and went down to look at the sea. There was a fair north-westerly swell, with the surface wind at right angles to it at about 8 mph. I decided that it was obviously possible to land and take-off again. We so reported by radio. I think that it would have been very difficult, even if conditions had been less favourable, to have given a thought to the AOC's order about not hazarding the aircraft. We had used up quite a lot of fuel by flying at high power to the area, but we now jettisoned some more to bring our load to 700 gallons. Then down we went. Coming in low, into wind, across the swell at 60 – 65 knots and about 20 inch of engine boost pressure applied to give a rate of descent of 150 feet per minute, I flew the aircraft just over the water until I saw a moderate swell approaching from the left. As it came under, I cut off power and with one small thud, followed by a heavier one and a stall landing off it; we came to rest at 0817 hours. There had been three chances to land on the run in, and these had given us a good look at the sea state before the final commitment. Once down it was not too easy to keep the dinghies in view; they were flat and the Catalina sat low in the water. We taxied downwind of them and then came up towards them. Due to excess care to avoid over-running them, we cut the engines too soon and drifted back. The port engine was not too keen to restart, but eventually did, and then, with the port drogue out, we taxied up past the survivors, cut the engine and drifted back. A rope was thrown and caught and they were pulled alongside. The movement of the float caused some worry. Soon my crew had them aboard – six men who had been in three single-seater dinghies for sixty-two hours. Once they were aboard, I went aft to see them and give orders for the take-off. We had to be on our guard in case German aircraft came out from Norway to interfere, but none appeared. The next thing was to get everyone safely secured for the take-off; light food and first aid could wait. The aircraft crew were beginning to feel queasy. We restarted the engines, but owing to our preoccupation with the survivors we had left the port drogue still out, nor had we taken any photographs. The drogue was a bag-like sea anchor on a longish rope used to slow down and control the approach on water.

Two of our crew came forward into the pilots' cabin area for take-off, to compensate for the survivors weight aft. When the engines were warm, the aircraft was taxied at a medium speed into wind until a comparatively swell-free area of sea appeared ahead; it was about a hundred yards or so. I opened the throttles rapidly to full engine pressure boost of 52 inches applied and with the control column hard back we started on the run. It was then that the drogue must have broken away near to the rope's attachment, and it must have acted like brakes on before a landplane short take-off, for we soon reached 40 knots, speed increasing rapidly and at 50 knots, the aircraft hit a small swell, touched lightly again twice and was airborne at 0900 hours. At about 300 feet I began a turn and it seemed at once that the rudder was very stiff, perhaps locked over. At first I thought Jacko, sitting on the floor, was hampering the rudder bar with his shoulder. But kicking him did no good, so Jock Brown went aft to take a look. It was then he saw the rope from the drogue was caught between the fin and rudder. He cut the rope from its bollard and a second later it blew away clear of the rudder. We felt very chastened that our error might have caused disaster. We sent the airborne signal, adding "six survivors" to base and set course for home.

I remember that after I had been back to check that everyone was all right and that some food and drink, but not too much, was being given to the survivors, I was sitting at the controls with a feeling of deep satisfaction, emotion, and thankfulness that we had been successful. It was about that time that Mac came and stood in the gangway by my seat for a time, we hardly exchanged a word, just a look. But it seemed that all our time at Invergordon, all that we had lived through together, had been worthwhile just for that moment alone. I was glad to have him there at that time.

We had flown together in the face of Providence – but with the help of Providence. Then a personal signal came in on the radio from the AOC, "Well done!" We got the aircraft back to Sullom, landing there at 1410 and the Liberator survivors were soon on their way down to the hospital near Lerwick. One of the survivors was a Canadian (WO Contant), with whom Mac still keeps in touch and passes on the odd message from him to me.

(*Bandad was awarded the AFC for this action. The citation read: "This officer was captain of a Catalina whose crew volunteered on 21 July 1944 to take part in the rescue of six survivors of a Liberator, which had been shot down into the sea two days previously. The sortie necessitated landing in the open sea 540 miles north of the Shetlands. The survivors were located and, forty-five minutes later, Squadron Leader French took off, rescuing all six men. This difficult feat was accomplished without damage to his aircraft. This officer's shrewd judgement, skill and experience of seamanship, together with his practical first aid arrangements on the homeward journey, undoubtedly saved the lives of the aircrew members.*")

The end of our operational tour together as a crew was approaching – they would go on a bit longer – I had to count my time at Gibraltar in my tour. There were only a few more flights, including one with a landing in Iceland, where we were "stood down for at least twenty-four hours". Mac and I met up with two Soviet officers engaged in the ferrying of Catalinas, via Iceland, to the USSR (presumably to Vaenga). One was a Lieutenant Colonel and the other was a meteorological officer and there was, for a short time, an interpreter. We exchanged toasts until well into the night, Mac left earlier due to a previous engagement, and the meteorological officer left early, too. I was presented with a Soviet Navy flag (there was one to each Catalina the USSR were receiving) and I have it to this day. The Lieutenant Colonel also decided that although I had not flown across the Atlantic, I had spent enough time over it to become a member of the Short Snorter Club – a club restricted to those who had flown the Atlantic and you achieved membership by receiving a dollar bill signed by the member admitting you. If you were ever challenged on this and failed to produce the bill, then the drinks were on you. The Colonel had no dollar bill, so an Icelandic five kronor note was used instead. Finally, I went off to bed in the crew's Nissen hut and the Colonel went to his. About three hours later we were awoken – we had to take-off within three hours! So much for "at least twenty-four hours" rest. We got off, performed a reconnaissance on the way and landed back safely. I was not to see Iceland again for fifteen years.

Then, the night before I left Sullom for the mainland, there was a party and a visit to a dance at another mess. There, I danced with a very attractive girl from the NAAFI. On my leave in Shetland after the war, I was to meet her on board the new *"Earl of Zetland"*, in passage from Unst to Lerwick and I introduced her to my wife. She suddenly said, with an impish smile, "Do you still do much dancing?" As I had never done much while on leave during the war, this question caused some surprise and some not very convincing explanation!

Next morning, with a load of passengers, I set off to fly a Catalina down to Alness. But before we left Sullom Voe, we did a mild beat-up of the camp, including the release of Government Property streamers (toilet rolls) and 'other articles' (condoms), obtained from the Medical Officer, and filled with a mixture of red ink powder and water which burst on impact! A direct hit was claimed on the Met Office. My second pilot on this occasion and who joined in the 'operation' with enthusiasm was Flight Lieutenant Tubby Wraight, later in the year to be lost on operations, missing on a patrol.

CHAPTER ELEVEN

Flying a desk

Once away from Sullom Voe, there was the slight chance that I would be required to go to North Russia, but this proposed post did not materialize and instead I moved into the Air Ministry to work in TO2 – the operational training branch dealing with Coastal Command training. We were housed in Kingsway in Princes/Alexandra House and worked under the lively Wing Commander Irving. I was to take the place of Squadron Leader Bunting, who had gone to the Staff College. One of the tasks was the weekly return of aircrew requirements for the various training units, including the Bahamas. Like many things that are new, this seemed a formidable task, until one found out that should you be away at a meeting or for some other reason, the Wing Commander's clerk, Joanne Adams and her friend Pam, were entirely capable of doing the intricate return and sending off the documents. Joanne, who was a smart, cheerful and beautiful girl, set herself a very high standard of work. Letters would arrive promptly on one's desk, already filed and with preceding correspondence neatly flagged and very often a resume of what had gone and what was needed now.

Soon, my wife and Sally had settled down in our small furnished flat belonging to our friends John and Joan Roberts. He was manager of the New Statesman, up in Lincolns In Fields, and was at the time introducing the Ganymede range of prints from his Great Turnstile office. Our rent was £2 2s per week, in Beauchamp Place! In wartime, although Beauchamp Place had its share of smart shops still, in general the whole area around formed a friendly little village, stretching into Walton Street and along parts of the Brompton Road. It was not a long walk up to Hyde Park, where mushrooms could be gathered and mint from the abandoned 'dig for victory' allotments. Nearby, lived my mother's old nurse, Laura, who was occasionally to look after yet another generation when our daughter, Valerie, was born in early 1945. Valerie came into the world with the sound of V1s and V2s and it used to be worrying to sit in the office at Kingsway and look across London to see a great cloud of dust and debris arise and wonder how close that one had landed. We even saw a V2 disintegrate in the air. Behind the flat was a small static water tank in place of a bombed house and here a pair of mallards were trying to nest, descending and taking off like VTOL aircraft.

During my time in TO2, the *Tirpitz* was finally sunk; as part of my duties I had control of and authority, to issue ship recognition models. I had my fleet in a warehouse near Wembley and I calculated that I had enough *Tirpitzes* in stock to give one each to the crew members who had sunk the ship. But I had to seek higher authority for this idea and before it came to fruit, I had left the branch. Soon, Squadron Leader Bunting was back and another place had to be found for me to fill. A vacancy arose upstairs in the Accident Prevention Directorate (APD), under Air Commodore O'Neill. The main part of the Directorate was engaged in a statistical analysis of the reports on the accidents and there were very many; but I was to work on the remedial side, under Group Captain Saker, who was later lost in one of the mysterious Tudor accidents over the Bermuda Triangle. My immediate chief was Wing Commander Somerville Sikes. The two sides of the directorate did not at that time work very closely together. We had an office staff who analyzed the reports with remedial ends in view and we were supported by a team of Accident Prevention Advisers (APAs) who went forth to the stations to spread the word and get ideas. Their 'domestic' side was handled by a memorable character, a Mr Rowe, who was helpful and ready to get people what they required and was known, I think to his own delight and knowledge, as the 'whitest man on the black market'. He was very keen on using Cockney rhyming slang, but I always had a suspicion that, in fact, this was a pose and he was no real Cockney. In the main office the APAs reports and the accident reports were considered and various projects undertaken in conjunction with the various other parts of the Air Ministry, the Chief Inspector of Accidents – whose inspectors did technical enquiries into the more obscure accidents, the normal run were investigated by officers at Command Headquarters, the Ministry of Aircraft Production and, most important of all, the branch of Air Ministry responsible for Pilots' Notes – TF2. The staff included many good and experienced pilots and some first class engineers, but flying was not really encouraged and the APAs went on the visits usually by car. Accident prevention was a hard thing to sell to the squadrons, however much they regretted the toll of lives and aircraft.

My area of responsibility was all overseas accidents, other than those in the 2nd TAF in France, Germany and the Low Countries, a formidably large area with many different types of aircraft and units. Just after VE day, for which we had taken our four month old daughter Valerie down to join the crowd before Buckingham Palace that evening, I was sent on an interesting tour to the Middle East, India, Burma and Ceylon, returning through the Headquarters in Italy. I saw a great deal during this tour, although I was unable to meet up with my old school friend, Pesi Ginwala, in India. I also made a big mistake when offered a flight 'over the hump' into China, I said that I was needed back in London by a certain date. Of course, when I got back and spoke of this, I was told that the date was only a rough one. The highlight of the tour was to fly on air supply flights over Burma on Dakotas. The wing with whom I flew was commanded by John Grandy, my old instructor, at Akyab and noted Battle of Britain fighter pilot, officer commanding 249 Squadron, later becoming a Marshal of the Royal Air Force. One morning he invited me to go with him in the Wing's Expeditor to fly down to Ramree Island, where another Dakota Wing, under Group Captain Ramsbotham-Isherwood was based. The weather was threatening and we soon found ourselves mixed up with a lot of waterspouts over the sea. At one stage we were up on one wing and looking down at the sea, I could see the sea swirling in a vortex, I forebore to look at the cloud above, that was probably doing the same and we were in the middle. We returned to Akyab and made the journey an hour or so later. These flights were enormous fun, for not only was there an opportunity to take the controls, but also to see the weather conditions at first hand and the operating conditions off the forward airfields. When the drops were made, another Air Ministry visitor and I took our place at the big rear opening, the door was removed and we pushed out the load, some of it with parachutes, some in double bags – the outer one did not burst, even if the inner did. For all our lack of experience, we achieved a very creditable rate of despatch, although it must be said, that the rear opening of the Dakota, in bumps with no belt, was a slightly frightening position to be in.

Two of our big problems about this time involved accidents with Thunderbolts in the Middle East and Far East. They involved fires in the waste gate area of the superchargers or compressibility problems in dives. Some of the accident reports on the latter read like accounts of bomb sticks arriving on the ground and exploding, as one by one, aircraft of a formation dived in. Critical Mach numbers were clearly involved and I was soon to see the combined Machmeter and Air Speed Indicator instrument and I endeavoured to persuade whom I could, that this instrument was essential for the era we were now entering. Fortunately, plenty of other people thought the same, although there was some early resistance to one more dial in the cockpit.

There were several incidents on the journey. There was the night spent near Calcutta in an American camp in a former jute mill. I got to bed very tired. I woke the next morning to observe that the sleeping accommodation was laid out on the mill floor in a series of small enclosures with little fences between each, as in some banks. Waking late, I went along suitably attired to the washing facilities. I found it full of countless, completely nude, transatlantic allies, some shaving, some smoking cigars, some sitting and straining on an open line of water closets, whilst amongst this crowd wandered, completely unconcerned, Indian pedlars selling the odd newspaper, sweets and other articles. What had happened to the maxim I had heard sometime in my youth – never appear naked before the Natives? Shades of the Raj!

At lunch time I felt I had recovered my composure, for I was keen to get a good photograph of a vulture or kite in flight to make the basis of an accident prevention poster – bird strikes were a common source of accidents in those days, too. I saw one bird circling over the wall by the river. We were lunching in the open air, so I went over with my camera to find that my quarry was with others examining a corpse on the mud of the river. I called over an American friend, "was this a usual sight?" He didn't seem to enjoy his dessert too much.

In Calcutta, I met up with Wing Commander Chabot, an ex-RFC pilot, and later he came to the Air Ministry to work with us. He was excellent company. The last night in Calcutta, I spent in a night club with some other officers and three of us gave a rather unsuccessful performance in the band. I can't remember what my instrument was. Later, returning to my room, shared with others at a boarding house, I was surprised to find a very wide-awake parrot flying about the room. I woke up several guests to find out if they were concerned, as owners of the bird. At last one admitted ownership, but a lack of concern. Early next morning with a rather heavy head, I went to the airport, where I struck up a conversation and had a much needed cup of coffee with General Mansbergh, while we awaited our respective aircraft.

This journey had given me many opportunities to fly in different types of aircraft, including the Ensign, and to see battlefields of North Africa, something of Palestine, Iraq and Egypt and to see a lot of wrecked German aircraft.

On return, I found that Air Commodore O'Neill was to be replaced soon by Air Commodore A. C. Sharp, who had been the commander designate of 'Tiger Force', the RAF's proposed bomber force against Japan. He was to sweep through the APD set-up like a whirlwind. In a short time, in place of the occasional Anson flight or the use of a Metropolitan Communications Squadron Proctor from Hendon, a fleet of operational aircraft was to be made available for the APAs and also for staff members: A Spitfire IX, a XIV and a XIX (Griffon); two Mosquito aircraft (VI and PR34); one Proctor; one Auster; the use of an Oxford, and there was an unserviceable P38 Lightning, the gift of an American General to the Air Commodore. Unfortunately, the last remained unserviceable and I got no further than a study of Pilot's Notes and some time spent in the cockpit getting used to the layout. But the opportunity was there and to be taken, to convert onto the others, when they arrived. Rather later on, we were promised that we would have a Hornet F1. There was also the opportunity to take a short jet course on Meteors. (One of these courses had been taken earlier by a member of the Directorate, who had achieved notoriety by landing with his undercarriage retracted). I did my course in April and May 1946.

First of all, however, in December 1945, I went down to Keevil, near Bath and was given dual in a Harvard, followed by a solo in it and then two trips on a Mustang. The Harvard dual was confined to circuits and landings, no aerobatics or spinning were done. I found that it was a delightfully laid out aircraft, very precise in its handling. Although I had loved the Catalina, not even its most fervent admirer could say that the instrumentation and control layout was ideal. Similarly, the Mustang layout (it was also a product of North American) was beautifully neat and precise. The first take-off in it from Keevil was a bit of a surprise, with no tendency to swing and no war load, there was remarkable acceleration and I was really unaware of what was going on until about a couple of miles from the start of the take-off run. But subsequent take-offs were under control and I felt very much at home. Next day I made a flight in a Spitfire XIV with the five-bladed propeller driven by the more powerful Griffon engine; one had to look out for the swing on take-off. Unfortunately I had some brake trouble and had to cut short the sorties. A week later, I went down to Northolt to try the Spitfire IX for the first time, this was much easier. I celebrated the New Year with a flight at Felixstowe in a Seaford with Squib Squire. In February, in spite of some indifferent weather, I got in a few Spitfire hours, mainly on the Mark IX, but there was one trip on the Mark XIX (another Griffon engined variant), in this I planned to go up to East Fortune, on the coast near Edinburgh. I ran into very bumpy weather and, somewhere south of Lincoln, I noticed very heavy cloud ahead and it was lowering. I decided to turn back, to find that it had closed in behind me, so I detoured around the Southend area and went back to Northolt via the Thames. Next day, going through the daily accident signals, I found that a Lancaster had broken up in the air a few miles ahead of, and a minute or two after, the position and time that I had turned back. Later, I was to fly another Griffon-engined variant, the Seafire 46 with counter-rotating airscrews, a preparation for the Shackleton engine layout that I was later to fly.

In early March I made a visit to Germany, taking a number of staff in an Oxford, for now Germany was in my province as well. This was also an opportunity to look at various German aircraft types, both in Germany and later in Farnborough. Christopher Hartley had been engaged in the ferrying and testing of some of the latter (including the Junkers Ju88 now in the RAF Battle of Britain Museum), after his night fighter and anti-V1 flying. At Felixstowe I had been able to see the Bv138 flying boat, the German rival to our Catalinas.

After the visit to Germany, I began my conversion onto the Mosquito. I did three circuits at Benson on a Mosquito III trainer and a week later sat beside Squadron Leader Bell Syer when he flight tested 'our' Mosquito VI on a circuit and general flying. Then I took it up. In April, I did some more time on the Mosquito and gave my new Deputy Director Group Captain A. F. Anderson (Andy), some dual on the Oxford, in preparation for the arrival of the Hornet. The next event in April was fairly hilarious, together with Ian Macdougall, an experienced fighter and Battle of Britain pilot, we set off one Sunday in the Auster from Northolt to Molesworth for the Meteor course. The procedure at Molesworth was fascinating. For those like Ian, if they had not flown on twins, there was first dual and solo on the Oxford, before they were let loose on the Meteor. Those who had flown twins, in general the non-fighter pilots, had the same initial lectures, drew the fuel system and off we went down the none too long runway (1200 yds) at Molesworth. But at that time there was no dual of the Meteor available, so this was the only way. On one engine the light Meteor III was a very respectable performer, so it was difficult to see why our faster fighter brothers could not have done the same as we. Further flights followed, including an exhilarating low flying session; a climb to 25,000 feet and finishing up with formation – a total of some five hours in all.

By the end of May the Hornet had arrived and Andy and I drove to Northolt to do our first trips. As we turned the corner of the hangar, there was a sleek and beautiful aircraft awaiting us. Andy made a typical remark, "I don't know about you, Froggie, but I think we should go straight back to London." We both made our first solos on the type and I was certainly delighted with it. My next trip on it was some weeks later, when I went on a visit to Boscombe Down to discuss some Mustang accident problems. There, I found Pop Sewell (Squadron Leader K. J. Sewell AFC, DFM), an old friend from South Cerney days, now a test pilot. John Newton Chance has described Pop in his 'Yellow Belly', but I must add a few words. Pop was a cheerful and indefatigable Yorkshireman. He had a habit of whipping off your mackintosh to see if you had been promoted, or the reverse, without his knowledge, for in those days officers' mackintoshes shoulder straps bore no badges of rank. Off came my mackintosh, in which I quite often flew if it was likely to rain on arrival. We went from his office to the Mess. When time to go home arrived, Pop had not asked and I hadn't told him in what aircraft I had come down. We came out on to the airfield for me to book out at the Watch Office and there was the Hornet.

Pop said, "That must be the Hornet I'm expecting for special tests."

It gave me great 'one-upmanship' pleasure to casually inform him that it was my staff visit chariot, and of course, he took this information with delight. Pop was to die not long afterwards, in a Pembroke with an engine on fire in the air, near Andover. The reports in the paper said that he avoided buildings to save lives and lost his own. That would have been typical of that good, honest character.

Meanwhile, Bobby Sharp was working on various plans he had arranged for some accident prevention films to be made. Already, for some time in our publicity, we had used the "Fly with Prudence" posters and articles and for this, Ruth Walker of the WRAF was our artist and did a very good job. Now Prudence, with Patricia Cutts in the role, was to go on film. David Moir, an ex-Pathfinder squadron leader, was in charge of the project and the studio filming was done at Merton Park Studios. The film showed the influence of various irritant factors – tiredness, irritability etc. – which could cause accidents, whether they operated on flying or were ground staff. One scene was to be an Officers' Mess dance. The film company laid on a shooting programme to cover two days, starting at 0730 each day; dancing partners were provided by the company, while members of the APD staff were to 'act' as officers. With great foresight I and a few others, including Johnny Onions, an ex-Blenheim pilot who worked with me, went down for the first day. The film company also provided 'live' drinks, in sufficient supply; it was thought, for two days. We had an excellent day's filming, dancing with very pleasant partners, a lunch on the film company at a nearby hotel, with more refreshment. We acted excellently, but those who had volunteered for the next day's work got only soft drinks, for we had finished the budgeted alcoholic ones in our one day's work. In the end, very few feet of our well acted work appeared in the final film. The flying for the film was done on various aircraft and one sequence, made on an unserviceable aircraft by Squadron Leader Nunn, one of our pilots, of a wheels up landing on a Mosquito, was excellent. There is an awful moment as the aircraft comes to a standstill, when the sun flashes on the opening emergency exit and it looked for all the world as if the whole thing was about to go up in flames. David worked on a film about a Lancaster also – this on the troubles of engine failures. It was ironic that a few months after leaving the Directorate, David died in a Lancaster accident which occurred in circumstances very similar to those in his scenario.

The engineering side of our staff included among others, Flight Lieutenant Ross, who fought long and hard battles with Ministry of Aircraft Production (MAP) on various projects, including improved flexible hoses and better tyres. He had many difficulties in the latter field. The problems were well known. One day a set of clear and horrific pictures came in which showed only too well the dangers from tyre failure and Flight Lieutenant Ross was able to make his point with considerable force and with results.

Bobby Sharp had a difficult time to get our office accommodation put to rights. The building had suffered from the blast of a V1 which had landed at the end of Kingsway in mid 1944, and there was little glass left in its windows for a long time – board had been used to replace it. But the only occasion I saw him a bit non-plussed was when I was in the office with him and a Works and Buildings man came in about furniture. Bobby described what he wanted – good class chairs, tables, carpets and so on for the important people who came to see him. The W & B man leaned forward and slowly knocked his pipe out into the Air Commodore's rather magnificent cut-glass ashtray and said,

"Air Commodore, I could not possibly sanction that!" I thought there would be an explosion, but there wasn't.

On another occasion, I flew down to the West Country in the Mosquito VI to collect Bobby from leave. The Mark 34, with its greater capacity, had been specified and as I came into the circuit, Air Traffic called, "The Air Commodore is asking why you have brought the VI?" I replied that the Mark 34 was unserviceable. On the ground there was a certain amount of doubt as to whether his golf clubs would fit in with the rest of the baggage, but they did. He flew us back to Bovingdon with me as navigator. Bobby was then very keen on the policy that the second occupant should always call out the airspeed on the approach to land. His approach speed was fairly high and as I called out the speeds, I must have introduced a note of interrogation, for he gave me an old fashioned look!

Later on, he took the Hornet on a long distance flight to the Middle and Far East which required extensive use of the drop tanks. If these were jettisoned there was a breakaway glass tube that had to be replaced and therefore spares had to be carried. Needless to say, in accordance with fate, no spares were available. So I went to Baird and Tatlock's, the scientific instrument people next door in Kingsway, with a sample tube and got them to provide some. I was, all the same, relieved when the Air Commodore got back safely from his flight.

One day I was air testing the Mosquito 34 after an inspection and on the air test, the propeller which I had feathered, failed to unfeather. The resulting single-engined landing was successful, although with no overrun on the particular Bovingdon runway, I had to turn rather smartly to the left onto the grass, this slightly strained the undercarriage. My passenger had been a young electrician who had worked on the inspection and I jokingly said, "That's what happens when there's an electrical fault!" The poor lad was out of the aircraft in no time at all and away.

We occasionally loaned one of our aircraft to pilots in the operational and training directorates. One day I was told by the Air

Commodore that Wing Commander Wykeham-Barnes (later Air Marshal Sir Peter Wykeham), one of the leading Mosquito pilots of the war, was to borrow one of our Mosquitos. "Take a copy of the relevant Pilot's Notes down to him, will you?" I did so, but felt that, with my few hours on Mosquitos, I was taking accident prevention just a little too far in this case!

Princes House was notable for one character, Danny the lift man. His handling of the lift was that of a fighter pilot with élan, but one day after lunch, he brought a full load of passengers up to the eighth floor and then prepared to go down. The doors were closed with a crash and then he selected 'up' and disappeared into the roof area with a cry of "——it!" He remained there for two hours or so, until they came to release him.

The time in APD was a most interesting one. There were various ways in which we achieved successes; one of the most fruitful ways was our work and discussion with the Pilot's Notes people, although they must take the credit. The period saw the early development of checklists, from the ATA notes, to extracts from Pilot's Notes, either typed or written on a postcard (the French postcard), to the start of the present day checklist. But out of it all, to my mind, comes the lesson which accident prevention and health-and-safety people must always remember, unless a safety measure makes practical common sense to the people doing the work, you'll never get anywhere with it. This reflects the views and policy of Bobby Sharp, when he obtained aeroplanes for us to fly when doing our none too easy desk job and carrying the message to those on the airfields.

From APD, I went to the RAF Staff College at Bracknell and when the time came to leave, there was a signal asking for volunteers for Russian courses. Having started to learn Russian from a Hugo's book in the train between Langley and London in 1946 and not being very impressed with the postings which the 'ace' members of the (Staff) Course were getting, I applied and was accepted. While at the Staff College we had visited the Joint Anti-

Submarine School at Londonderry and I was fortunate not only to see advanced and other captured U-boats, but also to go to sea in HMS *Trespasser*. Here, I found that life in a submarine crew was very similar to that in the smaller aircraft crew, with everyone feeling responsibility for one another. I was particularly interested to find that I could easily see the searching aircraft through the periscope. In fact, the whole voyage showed me that we had probably been more visible to the U-boats during the war than I had imagined. Much more came out of the Staff College Course, for we had an experienced Commandant, T. M. Williams.

The Assistant Commandant, then Air Commodore Dermot Boyle, later Chief of the Air Staff, told me that when I did things which I liked, then I did them quite well. He had got me weighed up. There were some interesting people on the course and on the directing staff. We had an excellent programme of lecturers, including Professor Jones, on the radio warfare of the war and Christopher Hartley. We also had some good visits. But it was certainly hard work, especially in the initial few weeks.

CHAPTER TWELVE

Paris and Poland

So it was that I arrived at the School of Slavonic and Eastern Studies of the London University in early 1948 and began the course of study. We were mainly an RAF course with two Army officers and under our three instructors passed our initial examination and then some of us were sent to Paris to develop our spoken Russian, while living with Russian families. Providing one did not meet one's fellow students too often and fall into the error of speaking English, this scheme was good. We would meet once a week at the Embassy to draw our allowances and this usually coincided with my host's vodka making day. The vodka was made by careful dilution of absolute potable spirit, from the chemist, with water and had the advantage that the more esoteric flavours (eg blackcurrant leaves), which required alcohol infusion to get the colour right, could be made. But it meant that my attendance at the Embassy was always a little light-headed. The time spent in Paris was, needless to say, fascinating, but certainly, highlights were to learn of the beauty of the Russian Orthodox service, especially at Easter. Followed by a return to the celebrations in a Russian home and then a walk back through the night to the house where I was living, through the Bois de Boulogne – with nightingales singing. A similar walk on another hot night was to take me past the bakers in the Rue de la Fontaine where the completely nude baker could be seen preparing the dough for the morning bread. Paris itself is a city to be walked through and enjoyed on foot. One of the greatest natural history triumphs was to find a kingfisher nesting in a drain hole opposite the Eiffel Tower.

I decided to keep my flying up while in France, so I obtained a French civil licence and went out in the bus from Versailles to Toussus-le-Noble along with Vera, who was giving me Russian lessons. Here, they had Norecrin 1203 aircraft, a light three seater with retractable tricycle undercarriage. The dual check on my flying was carried out in French by the instructor, the instructions were monitored by Vera in the back seat (she had never flown before) and passed to me in Russian. I received them bilingually and in this way we did a few landings and then Vera and I were off on our own. I made several flights during the months that I was in Paris; one of the most memorable was to take a small girl with whooping cough up to 10,000 ft for half an hour. The flight seemed to cure the whooping cough, but the bus journey to Toussus-le-Noble from Versailles was a little lively, as the small girl's coughing attracted the attention of the other mothers in the vehicle. Before a flight with Vladmir Brandt, another of my teachers and a new *émigré*, we watched a magnificent show of aerobatics by a famous French pilot on his pre-war parasol aeroplane fighter.

While in France, we also went to one of the early Orly air shows, later to become the annual Paris Show at Le Bourget. At this time, both in England and France, there were many exciting prototypes flying, ranging from the DH 108, Comet, Canberra and the little Saro jet flying boat in England, to the Ouragan, Armagnac and Bregeut Deux-Ponts in France. At this particular air show, a witty member of the crowd called out as a partridge winged its way over the field, scared by the roar of some jet, *"Ah, c'est un perdrix a reaction!"*

Eventually, the time in Paris came to an end, we returned and passed our examination and then the matter of postings arose. I was invited to take the post of the Assistant Air Attache in Warsaw. My predecessor, Peter Dobree-Bell, with who I had been at CFS in 1940, had had to leave in a hurry after being involved in a car accident, when a pedestrian was fatally injured. After a description of the job, I was asked if I had any points. "Yes," I said, "you'll have to get me taught to drive a car."

Air Attaches were controlled by an Air Ministry branch called AFL1 headed by J. B. Hogan, who once said, "Warsaw, Warsaw; it gives me more headaches than any other capital!" He got another Warsaw headache with my driving. But his staff were remarkable people, who did all in their power to arrange briefings before departure, to make sure that Air Attaches were supplied with all their needs. Eileen Davis (a war widow) for example, would look after children who had to be sent out to their parents for school holidays; travel arrangements would be made. AFL1 was a branch which could have no detailed description of its work. It put its hand to every task with good humour and got results. We began to run short of tyres for one of our cars in Poland, as large horseshoe nails could wreck a complete tube, so such a nail was sent back, attached to the request for urgent replacement tyre and tubes. AFL1 used the sample to good effect and we got our tyres in double-quick time. I had a very full briefing, visiting Rolls Royce and De Havillands where I saw the prototype Comet I on early flight trials – it was magnificent to see how John Cunningham handled it on the circuit and landing.

But I still had to learn to drive. The first suggestion was that I should do this on embarkation leave, but this struck me as a bit nebulous. What if I failed the test? So I proposed that I should be trained at the RAF School of Driving. This was soon put in hand by AFL1 and I went up to RAF Weeton, near Blackpool. The course took about a week and was good and thorough. Every day some 300 vehicles of various types drove out of the gates and on to the roads in and around Blackpool. While they held refresher courses for MT officers, they had never trained an officer ab initio (from scratch), so there was to be an assessment problem at the end of the course. The instructors were ex-police instructors and were excellent; we had a night exercise, a bit of lorry driving and skidpan practice and then the driving test. My assessment (I'm not sure if this was officially recorded!) was 'Squadron Leader French has reached the standard and is fit for promotion to Corporal', this was the sign of a good pass. Unfortunately, there was no time for the servicing side of the instruction, other than in brief. I had a lot more to learn and much experience to gain. This, I got in Poland under the supervision of Don Darvill, then AC Darvill, the Air Attache's driver and once or twice I went out with the Military Attache's driver. Both gave me good practical advice, I always remember Don once saying, "If you'll forgive me sir that was a ——ish thing to do!" Small wonder that Don, after leaving the Air Force, took up teaching as a career and went to Canada. If one goes just on his methods of getting my grandsons interested in talking about their school work (and few people can) as a guide, he is an inspired teacher! Don also advised on various points on our own car and I twice decarbonized the A40 Devon engine, sitting in the drawing room, having brought the cylinder head indoors from the garage, where it was far too cold to work on it.

When I arrived in Warsaw with my wife and Valerie (aged four), the Air Attache, was Group Captain C. H. Turner, who was near to retirement and his return to England. He was later to return to Poland to attempt to smuggle out a Polish girl, whom I met one day in his office, this attempt, not surprisingly resulted in his arrest, subsequent trial and imprisonment, all of which took place while we were in Poland. The houses of the Air Attache and his assistant were some nine miles out of Warsaw and a quarter of a mile apart in Zalesie, near Piaseczno. It was pleasant to live out of the city. The Assistant Air Attache's garden was a nice one with a little wood, we had Golden Oricles in the garden in summer and one year a Hoopoe nested in the garage, bringing up a funny little family which stayed around for a day, learning to catch ants. Storks were fairly plentiful, although none nested nearby, in spite of there being large fish ponds and a plentiful supply of frogs just down the road. This ran towards Gora Kalwaria and on to Czersk;

to the south it became a very rough third class road, but there was a branch to Grejec on the Warsaw-Krakow road.

Before Group Captain Turner's time and before the Stalinist pressure really started, there had been an official Anson available for the use of the Air Attache. This had long since gone, but after I had been about a year in Poland, the airport authorities at Warsaw/Okecia airport found a pair of spare outer wings (now obsolete) in their store and we got a large bill and a request to remove them. The wing sections were brought out to Zalesie and I used them to give protection during the winter to cars left out of the garage. The local security police were interested in the arrival of these objects and my butler, Tony, was asked what they were. He had done his time at some unspecified date in Russian prison camps and told them jokingly, "The major and I are going to make an aeroplane and fly away to England." He was told not to try and be funny.

Tony and his wife Antonia were the first Poles who we got to know well after our arrival; there were also the people at the airport, the Embassy Polish staff, the Turner's, Wladyslaw and Maria. We also had a Franja to help to look after my daughter; she was a kind, gentle girl, whose wedding we later attended. At a later period we had a girl called Hanka for a time, a very short time. Her stay was cut short because soon after arrival, she announced that the agreed wages were no good for her and that she wished to be paid in coffee and other NAAFI provided goods, which would have put us right into the black market circuit. Apart from this, the next morning she left the bathroom door unlocked while taking a bath. Unknowing, I went in. I couldn't act like the tactful butler, who said, "Excuse me, sir," her charms were there to see. I retreated hastily, being no 007, and by the time I got home from work that evening, she was back in Warsaw and out of our employment.

Sir Donald Gainer was Ambassador when we arrived, he held an annual party at Christmas for the Polish staff, the one in 1949 was the last. It was much enjoyed by the Poles and I think they appreciated it when I allowed myself to be taken into the Krakowisk with Wanda, the Embassy canteen waitress, as my very strenuous partner. It was a most exhausting dance. Also in the Embassy building lived, in a basement, the Komisarczyk family, a very numerous family. The head of the family acted as a general odd-job man about the exterior of the Embassy. In the winter, when it was necessary to sweep the snow from the roof, he would ascend there, fortified by vodka, and I for one was always glad to see him arrive safely back at ground level.

The interpreter in the Air Attache's office was Fred Adams, who knew Poland well. He lived on his own and on one May Day was standing in the crowd watching the procession forming up. The authorities noted that the Post Office workers contingent was a bit thin in numbers, so a number of people, including Fred, were drafted into the party. Fred marched with the Post Office workers and, as he passed the tribune, saw his Ambassador among the distinguished guests – but he did not see Fred!

Sir Donald was succeeded by Sir Charles Bateman (and Bridget Bateman). I got to know him well and greatly admired him. It was said that he would never accept wine when out to dinner, but we had some rather special Chateau Margaux, then obtainable at a reasonable price through Saccone and Speed and he would always enjoy this at our table. They were good friends to us.

The British Attaches, unlike those of the United States, were able to travel anywhere in Poland, other than in the frontier areas, without prior notification to the authorities, and of course, we were not allowed to enter military land (*teren woiskowy*). Although we travelled extensively, the other senior members of the Embassy were not regular travellers, except to the fairly well trodden places such as Krakow. Things changed after a time when such people as Heath Mason and John Rennie arrived, they could see that to learn about Poland it was necessary to travel as much as possible and to put up with some discomfort. The Consuls and the Commercial Counsellor, John Summerscales, his wife and family, were also avid travellers. Mrs Summerscales (later Lady Summerscales), had reached Counsellor rank in her own right in the American Diplomatic Service, before her marriage. They did much to organize social life for the junior members of the Embassy staff. Although there was an extensive diplomatic colony in Warsaw, with particularly democratic spirit about it, in that senior and junior diplomats and non-diplomatic staff, mixed freely among themselves. The best way to get to know and to love Poland was to travel.

In 1949 there was a tightening grip by the security forces on the country, the police, uniformed security troops and the non-uniformed security service (UB) being active all over the place. One got used to being trailed by Citroen cars with UB staff in them; to be questioned by them at road blocks; to the traffic check points on roads leaving large towns and to telephone monitoring. Not all was so serious; I went to a book fair in Warsaw and had noticed that I was being discretely watched. Suddenly, I saw a Soviet book which I particularly wanted, the one volume systematic book on 'Birds of the USSR', I darted to get hold of it and my follower looked positively disappointed at my choice. At this time too, the RAF mackintosh shoulder straps were now carrying rank insignia, for me two thick and one thin stripe. These, in colour and form (as well as the coat), closely resembled the coat and insignia of the Polish police. One day, walking through the streets of Warsaw in uniform, I suddenly saw a junior Polish lieutenant approaching, clearly with a view to chide me for not saluting him. Suddenly, he must have seen the crown on my cap, for he saluted quickly himself and altered course smartly. I hope that he remembers the incident with the same amusement as I do.

The country was, to a certain extent, divided geographically, in that there were the large areas of former German territory which the Poles received after the war, but they had lost areas to Russia. These former German areas had been fought over, devastated and depopulated. There had been great destruction all over Poland too, but it was most noticeable in these 'recovered territories'. In them were garrisoned Soviet forces, the bigger towns were being repopulated and buildings were being recon-structed, but it was a vast task. Not only had the towns to be cleared and rebuilt, but there were large areas of countryside still to be de-mined, wreckage, and all the battered ironmongery of war removed. Even Warsaw still had big areas where there was only rubble in 1949, the Ghetto, and even portions on the main streets had still to be cleared, but even in four years, much had been achieved. By 1949, most of the armed bands opposed to the regime, particularly in the south-east had been cleared up by operations, but that Soviet-Polish border area was, one felt, still sensitive. The regime was concerned to bring order and normality to a people who, for the years of the war had concen-trated its efforts against the Germans. They now had to be trained to be constructive, but, of course, they found it very hard to accustom themselves to the pretty harsh realities of Socialist work discipline.

Group Captain Turner was succeeded, soon after I arrived, by Charles Lockett, who in 1939-1940 had been in command of No.226 Squadron flying Fairey Battles in France. He was shot down and spent the rest of the war in prison camps, including Colditz, to which he was promoted for his escape efforts. He continued these there and must have infuriated the Germans – he joined in on the glider escape project. He would on occasion describe his life in prison to Poles, official and ordinary people, and made a remarkable rapport at once. It used to be said while we were there, that a Pole was a person who had been, is, or will be in prison, so Charles' approach put him in an extremely good position. We used to visit Stalag Luft III at Sagan (now Zagan) – the notorious camp, where the RAF officers were shot, fifty airmen killed in cold blood after escaping and was portrayed in the book and famous film *'The Great Escape'* – to see how the memorial was being tended, most of the rest of the camp had vanished and it was not possible to locate individual hut sites. I do not think Charles had been 'stationed' there. On one visit I was 'accompanied' by two UB men and I showed them the memorial and explained to them why I was visiting the camp site, what the RAF had done in the war and so on. They seemed genuinely interested.

Charles was an inveterate motorist. I did not often drive far with him. He ran a Bentley, which he had bought to take out to Poland and was typically delighted to tell how he had been given some instruction at the works and how uncomplimentary they had been about his driving. He was full of enthusiasm for our job and it was good to work with him, he had a sprinkling of Russian which he had learned in one of his prisons, but was more at home in German.

On one occasion when I was driving him into Warsaw, we picked up a hitch-hiking Pole, slightly under the influence, who spoke German. Charles was in his best blue, complete with aiguillettes, he was off to some formal party at lunch time. To my delight, the Pole embraced him heartily before leaving the car, breathing vodka and some other more aromatic alcohol all over him. The other occasion was when we were paying an official visit to the doyen of the military Attaches, the Soviet Military Attache, General Ivan Kazak, a fine old soldier. The General asked me to enquire what Charles thought of the American Boeing B29. Charles was a bit non plussed by this and made some non-committal answer which I translated back. General Kazak looked at me and with, if not exactly a wink, an expression which I knew well, said, "Tell your Colonel that a good attaché must know not only about the other side's aircraft, but about those of his allies and own services as well."

I admired the General. Once, when I visited him on some matter just before I left Poland, he came in accompanied, not by one of his usual assistant attaches, but by a young officer who became very persistent with questions about the British Socialists and the Nenni telegram incident (Thirty-six labour

Party MPs signed a telegram in 1948 giving support to Pietro Nenni, the Italian Socialist who was standing in the Italian general election in alliance with the Communists). Why had they been disciplined?

I said, "No doubt for reasons of party discipline."

The young officer persisted in his harrying but General Kazak intervened, "The major said party discipline. Besides he is probably also busy." The questions ceased and I took my leave.

The day before I left Poland, Stanley and Mrs Fordham, as they were then, with their daughter, took my daughter and me for a picnic. They had asked us where we would like to go and I had said Zelazowa Wola, the birthplace of Chopin, which I found a particularly lovely and inspiring place, not too far from Warsaw. My day was made when we walked through the garden, we saw General Kazak and his wife also there on a visit and so I was able to say goodbye to them there, although I had already paid an official visit.

There were several pleasant people in the Soviet Embassy; the ambassador at one time was Arkady Sobolev, who had been in England during the war. There were some very friendly other staff, who tried, unsuccessfully, to help me get a visa to visit Moscow and there was the Aeroflot representatives, Mr Druba was there during most of my stay. We used to compare notes on weather, as our two aircraft, his IL-12 from Moscow, my Dakota and later the Valleta from Berlin, often arrived within a few minutes of each other. The Valetta was something new and we had a conversation when it first came in because I thought that he had managed to take a look inside, but more amusing because he said, "I hope that you will forgive me, but we've nicknamed this the pregnant English aircraft" – a reference to the rather deep fuselage of the Valetta. On one of the Red Army Day parties, he arranged to look after me and we spent a pleasant evening talking about all kinds of things. On one occasion our aircraft crew were interrogated because it was alleged that the aircraft had wandered from the flight corridor, which was not so, but would not have been surprising in view of the paucity of navigational aids. There was then little or no radar to check on the position accurately, only D/F (direction finding). Anyhow, one day we had one of these sessions of questions, which had to be restarted when it was found that the recorder was not switched on! (That was our surmise, there had been a sudden silence, an oath in Polish, a move of the hand and then repeated questions.)

The Polish frontier guards were very firm, but correct. One day a King's messenger arrived with our bag from Berlin, but had forgotten his passport. The Poles allowed me to collect the mail from him in their office, but would not allow him into the airport restaurant for the usual refreshment, in spite of his protestations that they knew him from previous visits.

It was in Warsaw, because of what I saw and liked about some of the Soviet officers and officials and the whole fascination of the East European scene, that I began to hope that, if possible, I should go to the Air Attaches office in Moscow; moreover to form a wish and in those days a hope far less likely of fulfilment, that I should get to know and develop a friendship with some Soviet people. In fact the first wish was not fulfilled, except in so far as in 1956 I entered the Air Attaches office in Moscow on a visit. But the other wish has come to pass, in a different way to what I expected.

I found in Poland (and it had been the same in the USSR), the whole campaign had involved the use of many, virtually un-prepared fields to achieve dispersal and the maximum flexibility. Poland had been described as one continuous potential airfield. But, there were also such operations as the use, by Soviet fighters, of the German autobahn near Wroclaw (then Breslau) in the later stages of the war. The Germans too had bulldozed a strip through the rubble of the town of Breslau, and then there were the flights to and from the middle of Berlin to the beleaguered headquarters of Hitler. Initially, the early jet aircraft were used only off runways, but soon after the big Soviet runway airfield programme got underway in Eastern Europe, the use of natural surface strips and roads by jet aircraft became more frequent and a standard exercise. The Swedish and Polish air forces frequently exercise off roads.

CHAPTER THIRTEEN

Poland – Some reminders of the War and Faith

The work as Assistant Air Attache had many facets. Early in my time at Warsaw we still had a number of unclosed files on aircrew of the RAF, still missing after the war. This was even after the very hard work and successes of Squadron Leader Rideal, who had been recalled. We could not add much to what he had already done, but one case seemed likely to be solved, if only we could trace a grave in the churchyard of a village called Sasino, near the Baltic coast. It had been reported that this particular man had been buried there late in 1943. One cold winter day, I was on the road with Larry McNally, one of the American Assistant Air Attaches. We were driving from Gdynia along the main road to Szczecin and were to turn up north on a small road towards the village. The difficulty was that the village was close to the prohibited coastal belt and we had no wish to ask for special permission to enter that belt, the measurement on the map showed that the village was not in the coastal area. We wanted to look at Sasino and if we drew a blank there, then we could try and get permission to try some of the other churchyards that were within the coastal area. At the time, there were rumours of special installations in the coastal area and as we came along the Sasino road, we saw the skeleton of a radar aerial against the skyline. But this was clearly a wrecked and abandoned German one, probably part of the equipment along the downrange coast bordering the V-weapon range from Peenemunde. Rockets and other weapons had been fired along the range and their trajectory and fall had been accurately plotted and tracked. It was not the only one we saw and there were here, as elsewhere in Poland, many signs of the battles of the later stages of the war. This coastal area had been traversed by the Soviet forces moving east from Kolberg (Kolobrzeg). All over Poland, and especially in the former German areas, lay wrecked tanks and all that remained of IL-2 Shturmovik aircraft, usually the wooden parts and the engine had been removed, leaving just the box-like centre fuselage section of armour plate. Some villages were just dead places and at night were eerie and deserted as one drove through them. One knew that this destruction was in the past, but you could feel that it was not so long ago. So these reports of special installations related to the abandoned relics of the V-weapon programme, were not anything new.

Sasino village took some getting used to, as the road got rougher, it was clear that the area was not often visited, the fields not yet tilled. We drove up to the churchyard, through the remains of the village. I left Larry in the car and walked up. It looked a hopeless task, the battle must have passed through this very area in 1944 and the tombstones were scattered and broken. I searched, as methodically as I could, each of the graves for a sign that one might be relatively new or unmarked and the one I was looking for; the church itself was locked, although damaged and abandoned. I calculated that there were four graves not from the village. We had taken time to get there and it was getting dark. If I could but find a piece of evidence, perhaps we could get permission to come back and dig, when we returned to Warsaw. It seemed hopeless and it was then that I went to the wrecked porch of the church and wished and prayed that I could find something. This done I took a last look round and there in a heap of rubble, broken vases and wood, close to the porch I saw a small, familiar object, it was the brass 'D' ring from an RAF Mae West life jacket. I dug into the wet rubble with my hands and unearthed a number of torn pieces of such a life jacket's fabric, including a label which looked as if it might have had a number still visible, or which could be deciphered by forensic means. I knew then that at some time there had been an RAF man there. All this evidence I collected to send to London for possible identification.

It would be good to end the story and to tell that this led to the tracing and confirmation that this had been the particular man's life jacket and that he had been firmly identified. But this was not to be, before any report came back from London, we had written to the authorities asking for permission to dig, but no reply was forthcoming. As it was, the story ends there in that little church-yard, with thanks for what had been achieved and a prayer for my comrade, whom I was sure, was lying in one of the graves there.

Poland taught me a lot about faith, for the Poles were themselves living deep in the Stalinist night, yet their faith was bright and shown in many ways. On one journey up to Gydnia to visit the Consulate with mail, I was asked to make a detour to a small town in the former 'Polish Corridor' to leave a parcel of medicine for a tuberculosis case. The woman's relatives, or she herself, had written to the War Office (from whom presumably she had had a letter of thanks) for help in the form of medicine which was needed, but not obtainable in Poland at that time. The woman had helped, I think, some seven British escaped prisoners-of-war during the latter part of the war, before the area had been liberated by the advancing Soviet forces by which the men were presumably repatriated. Later she had fallen ill. I expected, when at last I found the house, to see a middle-aged person, weakened by disease. In fact the door was opened by a woman in her mid-twenties, still not much more than a girl, but clearly very ill. At the time of helping the men, she can hardly have been more than seventeen. Yet she had done this incredibly dangerous, brave, and selfless act. I asked a few questions in my inadequate Polish about her health; I handed over the medicine and took my leave by saying, as best as I could in Polish, "Thank you from us in England," and kissed her cheek. I felt all this was entirely and utterly inadequate, for before me was perhaps one of the bravest people I am likely to meet in this life.

This encounter was typical of Poland in those days. One alternated between emotions of great depth to some very light hearted and amusing contacts, from great seriousness to extreme levity.

One event on a rather more middle plane was the illness of my cook, Antonia. She was elderly and a great worker, but one day was taken ill and from all external appearances was, if not dying, at any rate going downhill fast. She was a devout Catholic. After singularly little result from the medicine given to her, it so happened that the late George Ingle, the Bishop of Fulham, whose diocese covered Northern Europe, was visiting Warsaw and I invited him out to the house for a drive round the countryside and to tea. But I also told him about Antonia's illness and how I was sure a visit to her cottage would help. A Polish Roman Catholic priest would not have been able, at that time, to visit her with ease (unless for the last rites), without some danger to himself, and the local priest was not in favour with the authorities. On arrival George Ingle went to Antonia. She was indeed astonished, for I had not warned her of my plan and only told Tony, her husband, at the last moment. The two held hands for a moment or two and then Antonia spoke to George in Polish and he to her in English. There was no need to interpret, for although neither understood the words which the other was saying, the thoughts were clearly passing between them. He then said a prayer or two, she kissed his Cross and he blessed her.

Antonia was up next morning at 6am to cook my breakfast and never looked back from that day all the time I was in Poland and she lived on for another twelve years or so. In later years, back in England, George Ingle was a great help to our family.

*   *   *

In order to keep people, and especially the young, from Church, political meetings would be arranged at suitable times with transport laid on to take people to the meetings in Warsaw. However, things worked out that the transport and passengers would be at the pick-up points early and everyone went to church in Warsaw first and then on to the meetings. Poland is one place where I have seen churches packed full inside, with queues waiting outside, even in winter.

On the lighter side – I was driving back alone one dark and filthy winter's night through sleet and snow to our house, when I noticed a horse and cart with a damaged wheel or a punctured tyre by the roadside. The majority of the Polish farm carts used ex-German lorry back axles and pneumatic tyres, and, while this gave added weight, it made things easier for the horses and solved a lot of the wheelwright problems. I stopped and offered the services of the powerful RAF jack to lift the wheel, so that we could take it off and put on a spare. The offer was accepted, for the man had been trying his best with loose bricks. But with the snow and ice and falling sleet, the stone-hard edge of the road was slippery and suddenly the jack slipped and everything fell down again. Up to now all had been said in Polish, but for swearing English was necessary and I gave my opinion in very basic English. Suddenly, I was seized in an embrace and my companion himself said in English, "and I never expected to hear the beautiful English language again!" He was a former soldier in the Polish Army in the west and had returned to join his family at the end of the war. As we worked, he told me times were very difficult, but this chance encounter seemed to cheer him up no end. As was so frequent in Poland, we never met again, nor was it wise at that time for people who had been in the west to have contact with people in the Embassies.

One particularly saddening case was when I found on my desk, for signature, a letter to a Polish widow, who lived in the same village of Zalesie as we did, with a picture of her son's grave in a war cemetery in the west. Her son had been a pupil at South Cerney and I knew that he had been lost on operations only a few months after leaving the flying school. I added a postscript to say that I had had the pleasure of knowing her son. Would she like me to call? The reply came back "Under present circumstances, it is not possible."

Poland had various effects on me, it was partly the country, in places a bit flat like East Anglia (it was said that there was nothing higher from Lysa Gora near Kielce, to the Urals), but it was nonetheless beautiful, the skies were wonderful and in the south there was the lovely mountainous scenery of the Tatras. It was the little villages, the storks, the goose girls and their charges and the sound of the frogs in the early summer. The beauty of the Polish spring which hits one so suddenly is indescribable, I have a picture of the orchard next door to our house (where Valerie's friend Olenka and her mother lived) taken from our bathroom, all the trees and the ground are under snow. Then I have exactly the same view taken a month later and the entire orchard is in full bloom. The spring was also the time to await the return of the storks. One day the great birds would come sailing along one at a time along some ancient path, first one, then another, and so on. One year the weather let them down, some turned back, to return a little later on when the weather had become stable. But most of all it was the Poles themselves. This time of my life was the start of a most difficult period, but how could these difficulties of mine seem of any importance against what the Poles had suffered and were suffering? Protected by diplomatic immunity, although I was never too confident of that in lonely places on my own, we were not subject to the real dangers of the UB (Security Police). But one was living amongst a Stalinist regime and you would have to have been blind not to have noticed what was going on around you and notice that people disappeared from the scene. It was for some depressing, for the insensitive, it was boring. I felt and still feel, that it was a privilege to have lived there among those people and to have shared, in a minute degree, the life of the Polish people.

In 1951, while we were on leave in England, my wife fell ill with poliomyelitis. She had to remain in hospital in Cardiff, but was near to her sister. There was nothing much we could do but wait and see how things developed, so my daughter and I returned to Poland to finish our tour. On arrival in Warsaw, it was a remarkable experience to receive a telephone call from a senior Foreign Ministry official (a brave enough man in the war, as I already knew from his colleagues) to say how much sympathy they all had for us. Elsewhere, it would have been politeness; in Stalin's Poland, it was a further act of bravery to telephone such a message, when usually all that might have been done would have been a formal expression at some reception or a message passed on through one of our Foreign Office colleagues at a routine meeting. We also had much kindness from the Polish staff in the Embassy and people in the village.

Then there was E.D., who worked for the Embassy, but was picked up one day to be a witness and then to be embroiled in the Turner trial (this trial concerned foreign diplomats being tried for illegally smuggling someone out of Poland, including the Air Attache Group Captain C. H. Turner). E.D ended up for some years in prison, later to be released on amnesty, for indeed he was innocent of the fabricated charges, but in spite of his own trials, his own illness brought on in prison, he always sent us kind and sympathetic messages through his wife. A few years ago he came to England on holiday, he turned up at lunchtime and we had a reunion that I had only dreamt about and it was very moving and happy.

During the latter part of our time in Poland, near Christmas, diplomatic relations with the west in general had become rather difficult because of the Korean War and late one night I was sitting alone in the drawing room, Tony and Antonia were in their cottage and my daughter was asleep upstairs. Suddenly, I heard our locked iron gates rattling and then the sound of several people approaching the house. How had they got into the grounds? Presumably they had climbed over the gate. My first thought was that it must be the security police. No use telephoning for help, there would have been the usual inexplicable delays. I waited and there came a knock at the door and voices. I let them knock again and I realized that I could not but open the door. I was terrified. So I opened the door. And as I looked out into the darkness, the shadowy figures broke into a Christmas carol and someone lit up the little Christmas crib they were carrying. It was a party of men from the village, one said, "You look very white, Major!" I said that I might well be so and explained what I had been thinking. They had climbed over the gate. We all laughed then over the experience, but if I have got any grey hairs or lost any years from my life, this is one of the times that I did so.

I have written that humour alternated with emotion in Poland. If one took the matter of medical and dental attention, there were some unusual features. We had the Anglo-American Hospital in Warsaw, where there was an English doctor, a Polish doctor, Elisabeth Gielniewska (Betty) and Polish nurses. I once had a poisoned foot from a mosquito bite when up near Gdansk. The Consul sent me back with his driver to Warsaw to the hospital for treatment. I received straight penicillin and crystalline penicillin by injections, administered by a kindly nurse known as 'the guardian angel of Grochow', a suburb of Warsaw where she lived and where (rather unofficially) she distributed much needed medicaments from the hospital stock. This was, of course a hospital under our control, but equally, when we visited Franja at the local hospital at Piaseczno, the hospital was spotless and obviously a very high standard was kept. The patients who were convalescing were expected to take part in cleaning.

For dentistry we went to a lady dentist off the main Jerosolimska street in a tall war damaged building. Two chairs were in the surgery and when I first arrived there was a second dentist, a man who was later called up into the forces. Those waiting sat behind the two chairs; X-rays were done in a separate establishment downstairs. A crack in the wall let in snow during the winter. We had to provide our own filling material, which came out in the diplomatic bag and no doubt the spare was used in the practice. After the call up of her colleague, the lady continued on her own. Then while attending to one patient, the second patient would be having a cup of tea and vice versa. I had excellent and regular attention. One day while in Krakow, I got a terrible toothache and there was nothing to do but to drive back the 180 miles to Warsaw, in considerable pain from an abscess under the root of a tooth. I got to our dentist early the next morning and she decided to root fill the tooth. This was done patiently and without anaesthetic, it was almost painless but took quite some time. She would inspect progress and sniff the cotton wool dressing with some expressive facial and verbal comment. But this root filling lasted for twenty-six years and only recently did some trouble develop under it, requiring replacement in hospital.

At one time during my stay in Poland, Marshal Rokossovsky, the Soviet appointed Marshal of Poland (he was in fact Polish born), suddenly disappeared from the Warsaw scene. Rumours were at once rife, for the appointment had not pleased the man in the street. One rumour was that he had been shot by a senior Polish officer refusing to organize a Polish contingent of volunteers to go to Korea; another was that he had fallen out of favour in Moscow, he had been seen leaving Warsaw airport. Whatever the reason, the sequence was not without its amusing side. It came on the day of the celebrations for the anniversary of the founding of Peoples' Poland, at a concert by the Soviet Army Choir. Just before the concert began I decided to go to the lavatory in the grounds. Suddenly I was aware that, beside me in the next stall and on the same errand, was the missing Marshal Rokossovsky, but he was dressed in a plain mackintosh. I made doubly sure it was him and hurried back to our seats and whispered to the Military Attache, "You'll be seeing Rokossovsky in a moment." Sure enough, a few minutes before the concert started, the Marshal appeared, not in his mackintosh but resplendent in his full panoply of decorations. Apart from this brief encounter and a formal greeting at the subsequent reception, I never spoke to him.

At the same reception there was Marshal Zhukov (Zhukov was the most decorated officer ever in Russia/Soviet Union and was credited with being key to the liberation of Russia from the Nazis and capturing Berlin), then, on his way back to favour after Stalin had virtually ignored him after the war. Marshal Zhukov singled me out to drink a toast with him and we talked. I asked him, how did he feel about "you with your Germans and we with ours?" He said that he did not like it very much, at least that was the gist of his reply. One could sense the great strength of the man and how much of what has been written about his influence on Soviet soldiers is true. There was inspiration in his very appearance; his direct look into the eyes of those with whom he was talking. There was none of the cold look of the eyes of Molotov, who was at the same reception. Molotov offered me a cigarette; it was the last time I smoked and perhaps a good way to finish an undistinguished smoking career.

CHAPTER FOURTEEN

Poland – The Air Force Scene

I t had been a fortunate time to go to Poland. The Soviet equipped and controlled Polish Air Force was still armed with the Yak-9, Pe-2, later some Tu-2, IL-2 and IL-10 aircraft, with various transports, LI-2, C-47, Siebel 204 and other miscellaneous types including the ubiquitous Po-2, which was also to be seen at the aeroclubs, and the UT-2. There were also other civil aircraft, many of Polish design and construction. The main air force flying schools were at Deblin and Radom. But already there were signs of airfield development and improvement, including a big airfield project close to Warsaw. In the next few years there was to be a continuation and growth of this programme in conjunction with, and in anticipation of, rearming with jet aircraft. In the former German territories, especially near Wroclaw and elsewhere in Silesia, were elements of the Soviet Army and Air Force with Lavochkin fighters, various marks of Yak fighters, IL-10 units, a transport and miscellaneous unit and at Kolcbrzeg on the Baltic coast, a Soviet Naval Aviation element, presumably part of the Baltic Fleet. The Polish Navy also had an element from the air force near Gdynia. Finally, there was a Soviet maintenance unit for the Pe-2 aircraft near Torun. Soviet soldiers maintained the landlines through Poland on the main Brest-Warsaw-Berlin road and other roads. Although they occupied rather worn looking ex-German barracks, the troops themselves were smart. At one headquarters unit at Legnica (Liegnitz) there were Soviet airwomen. At that time there was some discussion about hair length for the WRAF (formerly WAAF) in England, and I added to it by reporting how the Soviet airwomen kept tidy long hair, without any loss of smartness. I hope – I never heard – that my comments were brought to the attention of the Director WRAF.

Back in the USSR the MiG-15 was in production and over in the Soviet Air Force in Germany there were MiG-9 aircraft. Very soon after I arrived in Poland, we heard from our colleagues there of expected MiG-15 and Il-28 arrivals.

As an Air Attaché in a foreign country, one soon becomes attached in spirit and loyalty to the air force of that country; this, even though our contact with the Polish Air Force and its people was almost nil. I left Poland at the end of my time there convinced that there was no better air force in what was now termed the Warsaw Pact Forces, than the Polish Air Force. The Soviet Air Force, such as I saw of it, also impressed me with its mobility. The main thing needed is to understand the philosophy behind Soviet Air Force thinking. This is different in many ways to that in the west. There is less sophistication, there is a practical philosophy related to the operational need of the time, simplicity of operation is important, though if high technology really is needed, then it is provided in a practical way. The need to be flexible and mobile (to change base quickly) is important, the aircraft must be capable of operating off natural surfaces, if the need arises. One thing which puzzles me is the insistence on detailed mathematics in certain fields of theoretical treatment of some problems and a slight, but now much lesser, rigidity in relation to the control of aircraft and the decisions of pilots. Cooperation with ground and naval forces has long been a cornerstone of the operational philosophy, but clearly Soviet strategic thinking is not confined to this; air superiority and the necessary air defence to secure it and the continued development of a strategic air force are important. At one time the Soviet Air Force found itself in the grip of a Sandys like situation (Sandys paper focussed UK defence policy away from bombers and fighters towards missiles), but this seems to have taken a back seat, both missiles and aircraft have their place.

In the field of aircraft construction, there is much originality of thought and various unusual solutions are sometimes tried (although this and copying were particularly strong in the pre-war period, rather than post-war). Generally, a simple rugged solution, capable of easy servicing, is looked for in design. There is a widely held theory that much copying of western design takes place. Other than the pre-war copies, there is only really the Tu-4 case, for which there were some very sound reasons; thus I do not hold with this view. So many operational requirements in the service and civil fields come out to the same general optimum solution, with an overall superficial resemblance. The Tu-4 was an exception. The Soviet Air Force needed to start a strategic air arm; because of wartime needs to concentrate production on what was needed immediately to prosecute the war, technical development and production techniques were more or less frozen. The arrival of a force-landed B29 Superfortress gave the Soviet industry a chance to dissect the B29, prepare working production drawings for airframe and engine, all equipment, electronics and radio and to build up an industry to cope with the new technology – and to quickly get the nucleus of a strategic air force trained, ready for the arrival of the Tu-16 and others. It was an enormous task and in my view brilliantly executed, mainly under the overall control of A.N.Tupolev. But it should not be taken as a precedent in judging present day Soviet aircraft such as the Tu-144, or the present series of transports. Of course, the Soviet industry studies the efforts of other countries' industries, but it must not be thought that this means any less original thought.

In 1949, there were many signs that control of aircraft in the air from the ground was rigid – as I had also seen at Vaenga in 1943. There, there had been a whole committee on the ground armed with Very cartridges and pistols. I also remember, in 1950, watching an Il-10 on approach to Zagan airfield, obviously too high, yet it seemed an inordinate time before the overshoot action was taken, one assumed that the pilot had been waiting for ground confirmation of his intention or even for an order.

From the experience of our colleagues in the Soviet Zone of Germany, we in Poland were on the lookout for the appearance of crates, for it was said that much, if not all, of the supply of jet fighters was coming in crated and by rail. Yet the first Soviet jets which I saw in November 1949 had apparently flown in, for there was no sign of a crate near the line of Yak fighters lined up. In the middle of this line were some lacking propellers and closer examination through glasses showed that they were tailwheel Yak-15 jet fighters.

But, for the Polish Air Force, we had to wait until a few days before the Air Day in the summer of 1950. On that day I saw a crate at Warsaw/Okecie airport. It was not a MiG-15 crate, but grey and something else. There began the wait to see what was to emerge. No child could have anticipated the opening of a Christmas parcel with more excitement than we, who awaited the opening of 'our' crate. Finally, there emerged a 'modified' Yak-15, in fact a single-seater Yak-17 with a tricycle undercarriage and various other minor differences. This aircraft was well demonstrated on Air Day 1950 when the Air Attaches were invited and was flown by a Soviet officer (Major Gashin) attached to the Polish Air Force Headquarters. But, for the next two years, there were no special shows to which we were invited by invitation; one I attended at Bydgoszcz, as a member of the public, resulted in our being escorted from the premises, an alert official having noted our car with its CD plates and the special yellow foreign number plates.

That winter, near Christmas, another line of crates appeared, this time by the new hangars at the new airfield on the edge of Warsaw. Again these were not MiG-15 crates with the rounded tops. Eventually, aircraft from the No.1 (Warszawa) Fighter

Regiment from Modlin, a grass airfield some miles to the north of Warsaw, moved in. A radar appeared, the appearance of a radar often signified the approaching arrival of jets – and a certain number of wheeler landings were being practiced on the two-seater piston engined Yak-7 or Yak-9 UTI aircraft. Finally, the crates were opened and we saw what appeared to be a further Yak-15 variant, again with a tricycle undercarriage. But it was soon clear that this was something quite new and different to the Yak-15 or Yak-17; in fact, it was the Yak-23. We eventually determined that it was armed with 23mm cannon. It was a nice looking aircraft and with flying getting more and more frequent as more and more were assembled, we were on our way. UTI Yak-17 aircraft also appeared. Then one day some MiG-15 crates appeared. Although we were nearly 100 per cent sure that MiG-15s would emerge from these crates, this did not diminish the excitement of seeing the first MiG-15 in flight, soon to be followed by others. As it came over Warsaw, it resembled a swift in that long high speed glide they do in the evenings on their arrival in spring, or before their departure in mid-August. Now every time I see swifts doing this I remember that first MiG-15 over Warsaw. If the Polish Air Force were pleased with their new aircraft their enthusiasm was shared by us!

The conversion to the Yak-23 and onto the MiG-15 seemed to go well. Although there was one report from another embassy of an accident to a MiG-15, there was never any real evidence to convince me the report was true. Presumably the pilots had had a conversion course in the USSR, for MiG-15 UTI (two-seat trainers) turned up much later, progress was rapid and it was not long before the Yak-23s were doing air firing practice and night flying was started. The general standard of the flying was high and there was a marked increase in bad weather flying. At a later stage some of the Yak-23s went to Krakow, the home of No.2 (Krakow) Regiment and then appeared at other airfields as they developed.

Interest was not confined to the jets, some Tu-2 had been delivered and some were at the school at Deblin. Later on, it transpired that these were the lighter training version with much less powerful engines. Polish Airlines had had their Il-12s for some time and one day we saw a quite large new biplane with a scimitar airscrew. This was in Air Force markings as a light transport. At the time, of course, (although I soon learnt that this was the An-2) I had no idea what an historical aircraft this was to become, nor how important it was to be for the Polish aircraft industry, which was to build several thousands of the type. Meanwhile, the Polish aircraft industry produced a number of interesting prototypes, both of gliders and powered aircraft, and a light helicopter. The work on these was concentrated, but by no means exclusively, at Warsaw. A helicopter factory was in building at Swidnik, near Lubin; the Mielec and Rzeszow factories were being renovated; most work on gliders was done in the south of the country and this was to grow in importance.

Meanwhile the number of MiG-15, including MiG-15 UTI, in the Soviet Air Force units in Poland was increasing towards the end of my time there. The IL-28 appeared in the Polish Air Force just after I left, as did the new type Soviet radars, which were mobile, rather than the equivalent American systems.

The big airfield near the Powazki district of Warsaw, which they had started building before I arrived and I had seen it grow up and become operational, was now in full use. At one early stage it was still crossed by a public road and then, not surprisingly, it was totally enclosed by a security fence. But, one night in fog, soon after I left, an embassy staff member, having delivered a friend home to a house nearby, got lost in the fog and suddenly became aware that he was driving on a road surface quite unlike any in the area in that suburb. Suddenly, at the 'roadside' he saw MiG noses! It dawned on him that entirely inadvertently and inexplicably, he had entered the airfield in the fog and had strayed inside. Of course he had no idea where he was – what could he do? He kept on driving and eventually he was waved out a gate and a short time later found himself in another suburb of Warsaw, on the other side of the airfield from his friend's house!

I made quite a bit of use of the Polish Airlines LOT domestic services; the aircraft used were LI-2 and the odd Dakota was usually used on the international routes and the IL-12. The company had had some French (Bloch 161) four engined aircraft and a number of small light twins from America, but these sat in an unserviceable row at Okecie. The domestic services gave a good, well flown and practical service about the country, with a general average sector length of 180 to 300 miles, the exception was Warsaw-Lodz which was shorter. It seemed to me that the standard of service was just what was wanted for such a domestic network, although frequency might have been increased, but probably this would have been at the expense of economics. The Polish trains were also very comfortable, and, of course, in competition with the air services. However, most of our travelling was done by car and one soon learnt a great deal about long-distance motoring under poor road conditions. These were rapidly improving, but the damage of the war years was not going to be repaired overnight. Winter provided problems, but once the initial black ice situation was over there were no enormous problems, none that a shovel and strength could not deal with effectively. However, starting in the morning could be very hard work and one soon became adept with the starting handle. We had to resort to an elementary form of oil dilution to make the turning over first thing easier. Punctures were common, but the Polish "katki na goraze" were an effective, if spectacular, method of pyrotechnic self-vulcanizing. One tube repaired by this method served for years as a swimming aid and the patch outlived the tube. I wrote that we had no enormous problems, but I still remember one day when one of our four-wheel drive vehicle's radiator froze soon after starting. We stopped to consider the matter, but up came some Poles. They took cotton waste on a wire, dipped it in petrol, held it in front of the radiator, invited us to restart and lit the petrol. The flames drawn by the powerful fan, went through the radiator and played gently over the engine. In my mind I was drafting the first paragraphs of the report to the Air Ministry DDMT on the destruction of a 4 x 4 by fire. But nothing went wrong and the trouble was effectively cleared.

The main problem was often where to spend the night. We carried a small tent with sleeping bags and a primus and food and water supplies. A bottle of whisky was also a useful addition to the 'household'. When there was no hotel, then one set up the tent. Personally, I enjoyed the hotels and the opportunity of talking to people and the food was often interesting and good. I have a recollection of one village restaurant which was not quite in the same category, but the cooking was still good. The menu was soup with spaghetti, main course pork cutlets with spaghetti and spaghetti pudding to follow.

On occasion when camping, a security police car would arrive and set up camp alongside, occasionally they would move us on. Once, they suggested (near Lublin) that we would do better to go into Lublin, but we had found no room at the hotel, nor at the University hostel to which we were directed. "Then why not drive back to Warsaw?" I said. We were tired and did not feel like driving the extra distance, some 100 miles, that night. They suggested that there might be bandits around. This was a surprise.

"Bandits? Anti-communists, I suppose?"

"Yes"

"Then they are not likely to harm capitalists like us?"

We went back to sleep, with our guards alongside us.

Once, after spending a night in a forest, my companion Sergeant Fineberg and I cooked our bacon and eggs and coffee over the primus and the unfortunate UB, who were less well prepared, had their cold sausage. Fineberg then retired into the forest with a roll of paper; after he returned the UB men went and inspected the area where the Sergeant had been. Satisfied that

Fineberg had performed in a bona-fide manner and had not left messages on the paper to those opposed to the regime, they returned to the Citroen and we all went on our way.

One hotel where I stayed was a bit of an experience. I was with Ronnie Mills, our Naval Attache, with whom it was always a pleasure to travel, we found ourselves in an eight man dormitory and there were very few facilities. The snoring (and other noises) during the night were uninhibited, rather symphonic and disturbing. At least after a night in the tent, it was pleasant to have a splash or a swim, without benefit of trunks, in a lake or stream. Don Darvill and I, on our way to Berlin, were enjoying such a swim in a lake when a party of young Polish women came along and engaged us in conversation and our morning swim had to last longer than we had bargained for, until they moved on to their work. But the record for me was a splash in the Odra (Oder of the famous Oder-Neisse [Orda-Nysa] line) on 01 November; that was just a little too exhilarating at that time of year.

Our official contact with the Polish forces was through the liaison officers of the Ministry of Defence. The relations were always correct and friendly, although little in the way of facilities was available. A visit to the famous bison herd in the Puszcza Bialowieska was talked about, but never came about. There was once a big party with the Ministry of Defence, but I was on leave at that time. I was sorry to have missed that. At the airport we dealt directly with the various authorities – frontier control officers, customs and the airport flying control staff. One of the Ministry of Defence junior liaison officers was Captain Monat, who always seemed over correct, it was quite a surprise to me, when, some years later after a tour in America, he defected. At the time of the Turner trial I was visiting the Liaison Officer and mentioned that some of the published evidence concerning a person alleged to be me was quite incorrect. A glance was passed at the portrait of Marshal Rokossovsky on the wall and I assumed from that, the local microphone (if any) was behind the picture.

One thing I learnt from the Polish Liaison Officers was their method of interviewing in a room with a desk, but clear of all but the necessary papers, if indeed any were necessary. Since then, I have made a point, whenever possible, of interviewing people with a clear desk. This has often caused remarks about a lack of work, but it is a useful discipline to keep an office tidy and ensure that order can be preserved. Although I am quite sure that in another room, my Polish colleague may have had a good, normal and confused desk!

I cannot say that the Poles in 1949-1952 were happy under the Soviet overall domination, nor under the stern rule of their own authorities and the UB. For us, they seemed to have an undeserved affection, we let them be swallowed up in 1939 and they had come to us and helped to save us in the Battle of Britain and given much to the Allied cause in the RAF, Navy and Army. On one occasion, when Frank Wheeler was driving our car somewhere near Gdynia, we skidded slightly and went off the road into a ditch. We had passed a line of carts on their way to market on the same road a few minutes before and I suggested to our UB 'escort' that they ask the people to help us when they caught us up or perhaps the UB themselves could lend a hand? These particular characters were not very friendly (in fact unusually unfriendly). All they did was to make some comment on Frank's driving – they could afford to laugh in a front-wheel drive Citroen. They went on ahead into the market town to report. Meanwhile, the carts came up level with us and showed little wish to help. Frank and I were talking and suddenly one of the men jumped off his cart. He said to me, "You're English, are you?"

I said, "Yes."

He turned to the other man in the carts and shouted, "Angliky." At once there was a rush and the men literally lifted our car bodily back on to the road. "Sorry we didn't help straight away; we thought you were someone else, as you'd got an escort when you passed us earlier on." He had been in the Eighth Army.

Meanwhile, the 'escort' returned and were surprised, as they could not understand how we had got back on the road, nor would anyone tell them. More often than not the UB men were correct with us – though not as friendly as with one of my colleagues who was a Polish speaker and under close surveillance. One of his UB men, on a fine afternoon, came and knocked at the door and said, "Major, it's a fine day, it's boring for us just sitting here, surely you can go out for a drive and we can go too?"

I did once help in the apprehending of a particularly unwise motorist who was driving drunk and dangerously and who struck our car and made off. The police were grateful, and, not unusually, the offender was sent to the Embassy to pay up for the damage. In fact the repairs had been carried out more cheaply than expected and so he did not have much to pay. For a few weeks I received salutes whenever I passed the police station in Piaseczno.

No account of Poland can be complete; there are so many interesting places to be seen, and, at that time, it was not wise to photograph freely. Krakow alone was a whole museum of a city; there were the salt mines of Wieliczka, the Mazurian lakes, Czestochowa, Zakopane, Lowicz, Zelazowa Wola, Nieberow, and the Baltic towns. Unfortunately, when I was in Poland the restoration of Gdansk and Malbork had not taken place. But in the context of immediate history there are three places which I must refer to – the first of these was Hitler's former headquarters at Rastenberg (Ketrzyn), known as the Wolf's Lair. With the disused airfield up on the hill over the town, one could imagine all the story of the attempt on his life as it had been described, with the flight away to Berlin. However, it was a bit of a shock to drive in at one end past no notices and to drive out the other to find that the place was marked as still being mined! Again near Spala – the former home of the Tsar of Russia, although one could not see the old house, – nearby, there was the extraordinary bombproof concrete shelter, built to house Hitler's trains to the

Eastern Front during the night, with power houses nearby. The place bore probably the finest set of anti-Hitler graffiti in Eastern Europe.

Another place which made a great impression on me was the battlefield of Warka, south of Warsaw and then still not cleared. It was a fantastic scene of battle, a mass of the vast ironmongery of war, a witness to the tremendous struggle that the Soviet Army had had to make, to drive out and drive back the Germans entrenched there, after the crossing of the Vistula. Although the awful horror of the Warsaw Uprising, the Ghetto, Maidanek and Oswiecim were there for all to see (I must confess that I did not visit Maidanek or Oswiecim, because I knew what had happened there), the greatest impression which struck me was at the silent Jewish cemetery north of Warsaw, at Falmyry. Somehow, that brought home to me so much more, the scale of the loss of human life, the whole appalling tragedy of cruelty.

Now, with all the rebuilding that has taken place in Warsaw (in my time the main new rebuilding was the Nowy Swiat and the north-south road and bridge), when I look at pictures of present day Warsaw, it is hard to recognize the Warsaw of 1949-1952.

It was not surprising to me one day, to read the words of the Soviet author, Paustovsky, about Poland in "Novy Mir" 6/63, page 116 – "Tret'ye svidaniye".

"And again there came to me the feeling, known to all wanderers – as if you have left a part of your heart in the country you have just left. But against all the laws of nature, you have not become the poorer, on the contrary, you have become the richer."

This indeed was the feeling which I had as, one evening in 1952, I sailed from the port of Gdynia in the SS "Czech" to return to England from Poland.

CHAPTER FIFTEEN

USSR Revisited
1955 – 1956

N ow back in England, there was the question of my posting, it was now certain that I would have to be living with a housekeeper in residence to look after us, with my wife at home with polio, which sadly became worse. So we settled down again near Sunninghill and not far from the winter quarters of two great circuses. I once collected some elephant manure into a sack, while in full uniform, near Ascot station whence had emerged eight elephants from a train journey.

The first possibility was an Air Ministry post in organization, with promotion, but the domestic situation was such that I was sent to a less demanding post at RAF Medmenham. Here, I could do quite a bit of flying as well, mainly in Ansons and Proctors. We took part in an exercise in Germany, which was a pleasant change. In this exercise we made good use of the Oxford aircraft, which at other times was being used by HRH the Duke of Edinburgh. It had a magnificent radio fit, which contrasted considerably with our TR9s of the old Oxfords of ten or twelve years before. From Medmenham I went to the course at the Joint Services Staff College at Latimer. Here, there was a good gathering of people from all the services and from abroad, including Teddy Donaldson, brother of Baldy, my original instructor. On completion of the course I was sent to the Policy

Directorate of the Air Ministry, but it was hard to combine the demanding work with the equally demanding home life, which was very tiring. Fortunately, a vacancy turned up in the Intelligence Department of the Air Ministry. Here the work was more hard in some ways, but more congenial and I felt more at home. The background was familiar, much of my work was writing and assessing and there was some lecturing which I enjoyed. We had an excellent lot of people to work with, headed by the Assistant Chief of the Air Staff (Intelligence) (ACAS(I)), who then was Air Vice-Marshal William Macdonald. During the Battle of France, MacDonald had a lucky escape whilst flying a Battle being chased by three enemy aircraft. Working for him was the best time in my RAF career. During this time there occurred the death of my wife and my new marriage and the kindness of him and his wife were very great indeed.

Each week I attended a committee chaired by a Foreign Office representative, usually Lord George Jellicoe or Reginald Hibberd. The committee was businesslike, but frequently not a solemn affair. One day one of the members referred to the French in connection with some matter and another member made a crack including the phrase *"Les Anglais sont venus"*, presumably to show off his French. Three members of the committee, the Chairman, a lady from another department and myself, broke into laughter after exchanging glances. All the others, including the unsuspecting would-be linguist, seemed surprised by this result, what was so funny? We could hardly explain that the phrase used was the French girls' equivalent of the English girls' – 'the curse has come'. Another moment to be remembered was when a co-opted member of the committee was introduced as "Carruthers of MI5" – and it really was his name!

In 1955, I was asked to go as a spare interpreter in HMS *Triumph* on her voyage to visit Leningrad. This was one of the first fruits of Mr Khrushchev's (the Soviet Premier) enlightened approach to world affairs and attracted much press interest and we were accompanied by press and radio people. Not being a naval officer, my main task was to remain aboard while the naval interpreters went on the various visits and functions. It was rather tantalizing to be so near, and yet so far, from the chance to go to Moscow and so on. The best event was the day when a large number of Leningrad school children visited *Triumph* and were entertained in true naval style. One of the children aboard that day was to be our guide when my wife and I visited Leningrad seven years later. We saw few aircraft during our stay, but one of particular interest was a Shavrov Sh-2 light amphibian, a fascinating little aircraft and already a bit of a rarity. The manoeuvring of the high freeboard of *Triumph* to and from Leningrad, through the Morskoi Kanal, was a nice piece of seamanship and it was also interesting to see the great shipbuilding yards with 'Sverdlov' class cruisers and submarines.

In April 1956 there occurred the visit of Marshal Bulganin and Mr Khrushchev to England. This was preceded by the first visits of the Tu-104 to England carrying General Serov, head of the KGB, to check on the security arrangements. In those days, it was usual for there to be British/Soviet navigator/interpreters aboard aircraft visiting the two countries, to assist in radio telephony and checking on the navigation. On this flight, Squadron Leader John Deverill, the Senior Assistant Air Attache in Moscow, was aboard and was invited to take refreshment with the General, including hard boiled eggs, cooked by the General himself on hot sand! On the return flight, which was captained by the Tu-104 test pilot A. Starikov, the landing back at Moscow/Vnukovo was made in bad weather with touchdown short of the runway. For the Tu-104 arrival at Heathrow, I was asked to stand-by in the GCS (ground controlled approach) caravan in case any direct instructions in Russian were required. I had a screen to myself and was very self-satisfied when I picked up the return of the 104 a bit before the real operator.

In the programme for the visitors, was included a visit to RAF Marham, with a flying display, including aerobatics by the

RAF Hunter team. There was a rehearsal a week before which I attended. I noticed that the visitors would have the sun in their eyes for the flying display, so I bought a couple of pairs of sunglasses at Boots. On the day, I flew up to Marham in the Air Council Valetta with the Minister, Mr Nigel Birch, and others. Among the Soviet party was the veteran designer, Andrei Nikolaevich Tupolev. I handed out the sunglasses to the two chief guests; A. N. Tupolev had his own pair. The display began. The Hunters, as I expected, made a great impression, for the RAF, certainly at that time, was the only Air Force with a full-time aerobatic team of such standard. Mr Khrushchev asked Mr Tupolev his opinion of the flying and that veteran of aviation was most complimentary. What pleased me was that the Soviet guests, who had had a rather heavy time at Birmingham and in the days before, seemed to relax completely with the RAF and enjoyed themselves. Mr Khrushchev issued a general invitation to those present to come to the USSR to see something of the Soviet Air Force. After the display there was champagne in the control tower and we talked. At the time, Mr Khrushchev was not yet so well known in England and one Air Officer, using me as an interpreter, asked him if he enjoyed making speeches at receptions and the like. I put the question, and, out of the corner of my eye, saw someone call the Air Officer away. Mr Khrushchev meanwhile was making his answer – "No, not very much."

Being alone with him, I said, "That's an odd answer for someone who spoke for so many hours at the last party congress."

He was a little taken aback, but then laughed heartily. He went on to explain that he spoke for so much time; then there was a break before the next section, so it was not so tiring. I asked him about notes. He said he could speak for up to forty minutes without notes, but needed them for reference, for figures and detail. He then introduced his son, Sergei, to me and we talked, all three together, about their impressions. His son had come along, he said, as he had done well with his studies. The guests also visited a married quarter and other places on the camp. Mr

Bulganin gave back his sunglasses on leaving, with a polite bow, but Mr Khrushchev kept his and I was glad he did. The impression I had of Mr Khrushchev was certainly of a man of direct character, a bit rough of speech, but open-hearted. He has been much criticized here and even more in the USSR, but to his everlasting credit, he opened up an era of more direct, personal contact between his country and others. Warts and all, he was a likeable man, with obvious interest in air force matters. I believe that an elder son was lost in the Air Force in the war. I had the distinct feeling that he liked the company of airmen and I am sure that his later interest in the cosmonauts was a very genuine one indeed. He was also keen to allow greater freedom in art and literature, although he would criticize freely and colourfully, that which he did not like.

The guests were later to attend dinner at the Royal Naval College at Greenwich, in the Painted Hall. This was also an occasion which they enjoyed, A. N. Tupolev was seated at the same table as me and we had further opportunity to talk and I introduced him to my chief, Air Vice-Marshal Macdonald. The other visitors included the late academician Kurchatov, the brilliant Soviet nuclear physicist, who was a charming person and whose lecture at Harwell is said to have been most impressive. There was a Mr Stolyarov, apparently Mr Khrushchev's personal body guard, who had been with him on many visits, including the attendance at the detonation of the first Soviet hydrogen bomb test. I said that I understood that had been a 'tower' test, but I was told, no, it had been dropped from an aircraft and this point was underlined in a speech by Mr Khrushchev later on.

The return visit to the USSR to see their Air Force took place in June-July 1956. Air Day in the USSR is in August, but at that time the annual display was earlier in the year. In 1956 it was made a special occasion with invitations to a great many world countries, as well as to the RAF delegation and one to the British aircraft industry. That delegation was headed by Sir George Edwards.

On the evening before we left, some of the RAF delegation met at the flat of Air Chief Marshal Sir R. Ivelaw-Chapman, who, as VCAS, was to be in charge of the party supporting the Minister. Next morning we set off for Heathrow, where the Comet II of No.216 Squadron (Wing Commander B. Sellick and Squadron Leader P. Bugge of De Havillands) was waiting for us. With us flew Colonel A. N. Konstantinov, the Soviet Air Attaché, known to the cognoscenti as 'Staro', after the town of Starokonstantinov in western USSR, which had an airfield. He said he was hoping to see his mother while in Moscow as she had been ill. He also told me that he hoped to get back to flying; he was fond of the Pe-2, regrettably for him by then obsolete. The other senior officers were Air Marshal Sir Thomas Pike, Air Marshal (later Sir) Kenneth Cross, Air Chief Marshal Sir Harry Broadhurst, Air Marshal Silyn Roberts, Group Captains (later to be of Air Rank) F.Rosier and Lewis Hodges (Commanding Officer RAF Marham at the time). We also had with us Squadron Leader D.M.Clause, who was Staff Officer to VCAS and the interpreter team of Squadron Leader Mike Forter of AFL3, a former Czarist officer and brother of the Russian in whose house I had stayed in Paris – Kostya Kougoulsky, Squadron Leader Ivanov (later Ivelaw) and myself. We had an excellent lunch during the flight with liberal supplies of caviar kindly provided by Colonel Konstantinov. We passed over Warsaw in the course of the flight and landed at Moscow/Vnukovo. Part of the delegation was only to stay a few days, but I was there for the whole time, which was very fortunate.

The main interest of the journey was to attend the Air Day Display at Tushino. Although, in the event there were other visits of great interest, as I shall describe. It is always difficult to say which year's 'Tushino' was the most important in this period, but the aircraft prototypes shown that year of 1956 set the pattern for development for virtually the next twenty years. There were the Mikoyan and Sukhoi prototypes which led to the MiG-21 and the various Sukhoi fighters, as well as the Yak-25 and its derivatives, still in service in 1978. There have been shows since 1956, notably the one in 1961 and the big show at Moscow/ Domodedovo in 1967, but there has been none on that scale since; nor have aircraft taken part in Red Square military parades for many years. The problems of organizing such shows become increasingly difficult as civil air traffic grows.

The 1956 Display was on the traditional grounds, the first part being devoted to a flypast of banners, aircraft, gliders and para-chutists, the work of the DCSAAF, the para-military training organization which includes the aeroclubs (Tushino is the parent airfield of the No.1 Aeroclub of the USSR); then came the Soviet Air Force sections which included individual and group aero-batics, fly-past by various current types and finally the prototypes. The procedure ended with a display by the Soviet Airborne Forces. The display was well organized and well flown. This was followed in the evening by a reception. A further visit took us to the airfield at Kubinka, west of Moscow, where a number of aircraft were shown on the ground, these included some of the less successful prototypes, such as the NATO desig-nated 'Blowlamp' Il-54, presumably to the same specification requirement as the Yak-28, the 'Brawny' Il-40 ground attack aircraft, and the Tu-92 anti-submarine aircraft, rather like a Fairey Gannet. The numbers, except for the Yak-28, represent design numbers, not service ones. But for me the best aircraft on show was the Myasishchev 'Bison', which might be designated M-4 or Mya-4, although the Soviet press has always given it the desig-nation of 201M. This aircraft in flight, looked smaller than it in fact was, when seen on the ground, it had beautiful lines and although modern operational needs have added excrescences to an originally clean aircraft, it still looks good. Myasischev deserves far more than the virtual anonymity for this creation. The 'Bear', that vast turbo-prop bomber (Tu-20), and later to be a general basis for the big Tu-114 Aeroflot aircraft, was also at Kubinka. The Tu-104 was also there, as was a wing tip to wing flight refuelling device which was later fitted to the Tu-16 and on which it is still used. The programme included an aerobatic display by a MiG-17 team which was good.

We also visited the Ilyushin factory at Central Airport Khodinka. The Il-14 production line was shown to us and there was an Il-28 or some other twin jet under covers on the airfield. We were taken to the Klimov factory, where the production shown was that of the VK-1F, the Soviet development of the Rolls Royce Nene. V.Klimov was there and we had a short talk as he recalled his visit to Rolls Royce. We were also taken to the Zhukovsky Air Force Engineering Academy, now much bigger, but then mainly within the confines of the old Palace on the Leningrad Prospekt, and to the Air Force Academy at Monino (now the Academy named after Yuri Gagarin).

These visits were all of great interest. The visit to the Zhukovsky Academy especially so, as we were able to see all kinds of detail, including radar arrays and engines and to see inside the rear end of a MiG-19 fuselage; all things that one had seen only in pictures or drawings in the press. In one demonstration room, the visitors from all the air forces were sat down and an aircraft machine gun was on the bench. Some wag remarked that he hoped it had not been loaded by mistake. In another room an officer was demonstrating a Geiger counter. My watch is not luminous and so there was no reaction from the instrument. "Never mind," I suggested, "wait until the Americans come in. That'll set it going." This simple joke was well received by our hosts, long surfeited with the propaganda of the Cold War, now relaxing.

At Monino we saw mostly the domestic attractions of this important Academy – to be Commandant of this is reserved for the cream of Soviet air commanders. But it is not very easy to show as much at a staff college type establishment, as it is at an engineering one, where there are wind tunnels and hardware. We were accompanied on this occasion by one or two unfamiliar guides and I asked one if we were going to see the airfield. "What airfield?" was the reply. Obviously not an Air Force man.

"Surely you saw the runway as we came along the main road?" Anyhow, after lunch we were taken out to the airfield and in fact were driven down the runway in the wake of a Tu-4 which was taking off.

We had some pleasant Soviet Air Force Officers with us as guides and interpreters, not only had they not spoken English in earnest before, but their teaching had been so good that they coped with very few errors. Apart from that, they were also good company and patient.

After the main delegation had left we paid several other visits, including one to Stalingrad (Volograd). We were flown there in Soviet Air Force VIP Il-14 transports from the Central Airport (Khodinka), which was only a minute or two from our hotel, the Sovetskaya. The morning was very fine and we arrived at Stalingrad/Gumrak to feel at once that there was southern warmth, although it had been warm enough in Moscow. The flight took us over the Don as well. The visit was well organized; we were given a room in a hotel for a wash and a meal and then shown the town, including the important buildings of the battle which have been left as monuments. A visit was paid to the Mamaev Kurgan overlooking the Volga; to the south-east lay one of the birthplaces of Soviet rocket development, not visible. Then we went to the Museum and were given a talk on the battle by General Sychev and Marshal Rudenko of the Air Force. The latter's exposition of the air situation during the battle was extremely good and clear, small wonder he had been one of the great air commanders of the war and a Hero of the Soviet Union as well. We returned to Moscow after a few minutes walk along the banks of the Volga by the port, where a handsome river steamer was at the quay, and another good meal. The flight back to Moscow meant that we arrived back at last light with evening falling and lowering clouds. We had had some very fizzy fruit juice in the aircraft soon after take-off and although I felt a little airsick, I was able to enjoy the skilful low flying approach over the city into Khodinka, which is only a few minutes by taxi from Red Square.

We were also taken to Leningrad, again in an Il-14 with Air Commodore Macdonnell, the new Air Attache, with us. Soon after take-off, we could see in the distance the early work on the new civil airport of Moscow. It was therefore fitting that our senior officer with us was General Loginov, later to be the Soviet Minister of Civil Aviation and head of Aeroflot. He was, I believe, a Leningrader and seemed very disappointed that we were only going for the day. We were taken to see many of the sights in a very quick tour, including the restored fountains at Peterhof and the Pulkovo Observatory, which had been restored after being in the front line of the ground battle for the city. This short visit added to my wish to return to the city for a longer stay, which had been kindled by the visit in HMS *Triumph* the year before.

In Moscow, after the Air Display, we had been to a reception which started indoors in the House of the Soviet Army, the big services club and recreational centre in Moscow. Marshal Zhukov was the host and in the course of the meal I had a long talk with A. N. Tupolev. He and I found a dish of crayfish which appeared to have been concealed by a waiter and we shared it with relish. Thrice Hero of the Soviet Union (then Colonel) Ivan Kozhedub and one of the outstanding Soviet fighter pilots of the war was there. I had recently read his book and so we talked briefly about it. Later, the party moved out into the park of the House. One fascinating meeting which I witnessed was that of Mike Forter and Marshals Budenny and Voroshilov. Mike and Budenny found that they had been in the same unit of the Czarist Army. The reunion was friendly, a bit different to what might have been if they have met in 1917 or 1918. In the park occurred the famous scene about which there were widely circulated reports that Mr Khrushchev was drunk and disgraced himself. First he took our Minister, Mr Birch, for a row on the lake. I found myself beside a seat on which Mr Mikoyan (the political leader, not his aircraft designer brother) was sitting. We talked and watched the scene. At this time there were also widely circulated reports that he, Mr Mikoyan, had shot Beria, the former security minister, and I had an enormous wish to ask him if it were true. As it was, he proved a pleasant person to talk to. There followed the session when the Soviet leaders sat on one side of the table in the garden and talked across to the various distinguished guests, or rather Mr Khrushchev did most of the talking. He greeted people by name and referred particularly to Group Captain Hodges and said how much he had enjoyed visiting the aerodrome at Marham. He also greeted and congratulated Lyulka, the engine designer, whose designs were now becoming very important. His wife was beside me at the time and seemed much moved by all this.

Certainly after some time, some of Mr Khrushchev's remarks caused mutterings by Messrs Molotov, Malenkov and Kaganovich, with suggestions that he should stop, but other than this, it was a good natured occasion, reminiscent of a cheerful guest night in the RAF, without the games and other slight excesses.

The Soviet authorities spared no effort to make sure that we enjoyed our stay. We went three times to the Bolshoi Theatre. I owe Marshal Sulets a beer from this. We were also taken one day to see the then new first Soviet atomic power station near Maloyroslavets. Quite apart from the fact that I personally had seen no atomic installation or technology before, this was interesting enough. But on the way a stop was made at the roadside memorial, not far from the place of her death, to the young eighteen year old partisan girl, Zoya Kosmodem'yanskaya. It was very moving to see this memorial, for I knew about her from my reading of Russian books. As we drove down to Maloyaroslavets, we passed an airfield, at which I was pleased to see some of the radar equipped MiG-17 fighters among the line of parked standard MiG-17s.

Needless to say, we also paid visits to the various sights of Moscow – the Kremlin, GUM and so on. While our chiefs were visiting Soviet Air Force Headquarters, the rest went to the Novodevichy Monastery and cemetery, where many famous people are buried – the victims of the Maxim Gorki (ANT-20) mid-air collision are buried there, as well as many people famous in Russian and Soviet arts and sciences, including Gogol, wherever one turns there is an historical name. On the way back to the Headquarters we went to a small private vegetable market, where produce was sold by individuals.

The other visit which was fascinating was to the Lenin and Stalin Mausoleum on Red Square. Lenin seemed rather remote, but Stalin's gaze seemed to follow one as one walked around. Whatever opinion people may hold on this embalming and preservation, it is certainly an experience to see with one's own eyes this figure of history – and I was glad to have seen Stalin, too. However, it was probably not a sound precedent to have included Stalin in the Mausoleum and it was as well to remove him to the Kremlin Wall. Certainly, with the less contentious figure of Lenin there, I could sense the importance, indeed the sacredness of this place to the true communist.

Then came our return to England from Vnukovo in the Comet, which had in the meantime been flown by A. Starikov, we landed back at Hatfield and the journey home from there took longer than the flight from Vnukovo!

The Soviet Air Force sent a delegation in September 1956 to visit the RAF and the Farnborough Air Show. They also attended an RAF guest night, which I am told they enjoyed. One of their number, Colonel Blagoveshchensky, flew the two-seat Hunter. As head of the Soviet test pilots school, no doubt he enjoyed the experience, but would probably have appreciated something else. After all, the Soviet aircraft industry, and, as witness to the conversion of the Hurricane to a two-seater in 1942, the Soviet Air Force, have long been adept at producing two-seater training variants of operational aircraft. But I missed this return visit, as I was away in the South of France on honeymoon, after my marriage to Vera. I served on at the Air Ministry until the end of my tour. Then I was posted, first to a refresher course on the Varsity, which was cancelled, and then was sent direct to a conversion course on Shackletons at RAF Kinloss. We drove up there and settled in at the Kimberley Inn at Findhorn. As far as the course was concerned, it did not go too well. But we were to see porpoises playing within the great rollers coming in to Findhorn beach; see the salmon netting and visit friends and relations. I had been too long away from proper, organized flying and, although I think something could have been salved, I was posted to the NATO headquarters at Kolsas, near Oslo, which proved to be a good two years.

CHAPTER SIXTEEN

Off to Norway –
Svalbard revisited
– RAF (Retired)

Embarkation leave was followed by a drive up to Newcastle and a voyage across the North Sea by Fred Olsen (ferry), to Oslo via Kristiansand. After a day or two at the Gabelshus hotel, we moved into a modern flat on the Bygdoy Alle, which overlooked the Oslo Fjord and we were there for nearly two years. During that time I worked as Exercises and Manoeuvres Officer, in a sub section of the headquarters, as the only RAF officer among USAF officers. My first Colonel was Colonel Maule, who seemed determined to make the NATO idea work and who seemed to believe that the American in Europe should avail himself of and appreciate what was best in this continent. I once heard him advise a new arrival who asked about obtaining American beer, "Don't worry about that horse piss, get to like the good Norwegian stuff!" His description of my duties was succinct and very clear, even if not entirely repeatable. My fellow USAF officers were a good crowd, friends to this day, but in particular, I learnt to appreciate the USAF NCOs whom we had – they were good ambassadors for their country and worked hard. I was lucky, too, to meet up with some of my friends from 330 and 333 Squadrons from Sullom Voe and still in the Royal

Norwegian Air Force. I also made many new friends, notably Gordon Ash and his family. Colonel Maule was followed by the kindly Colonel Gunn. Up the hill from our Air Force North headquarters was Allied Forces North, they had their own exercises staff, with whom we worked closely on the preparation of exercise scenarios and so on. It was all good inter service and international working and a fine chance to put some of the principles learned at Latimer into use, but now and again one had to stand on one's own point and hold it.

With fairly extensive free time, I applied for a Norwegian civil flying licence and flew Piper Cubs – in summer on wheels, off Fornebu airfield and in winter on skis, off the frozen Oslo Fjord. I had a little trouble with the medical, for a minor heart defect noted on my first medical after my return from Poland was noticed by the Norwegian doctors; I had two listening down the one stethoscope. They finally accepted me as fit, largely because I was so graded by the RAF, but suggested it might need reconsideration some time. The winter operation of the Piper on skis was very reminiscent of flying boat techniques, especially in the landing. Mostly, the take-offs and landings were made from ice with a snow covering, but when there was direct contact with ice only, then the whole process was much noisier on touchdown. The approach was made with a little power on and a set airspeed/attitude, adjusting power to give the required rate of descent. One could touchdown almost without noticing on some snow surfaces. A big advantage of the winter flying was the beauty of the scenery and the virtual absence of bumps, as the air in Norway in summer was often very turbulent for the light Piper Cub. There were a few seaplanes about too, but I was not lucky enough to get the use of one. A few others also took out Norwegian licences to enjoy the airborne winter sport.

There were endless opportunities for walking in the Nordmark forests north of Oslo; as autumn colours came and were replaced by snow, so one continued one's walks on skis. This cross-country skiing I found very pleasant and it required less skill than the slalom, which others who were younger took up. Some very fascinating bird and animal observations could be made, often with the aid of tracks noted in the snow. One rather unexpected summer observation was of the large number of snakes, which presumably spend the fairly severe winter deep down in rocky crevices.

During the summer of 1959 I decided that I must make a visit to Svalbard. My wife and her mother were to remain in Oslo and I would take my daughter. However, at the last moment, we found that our dates would coincide with a visit by my mother and in spite of her seventy-six years, she decided that she would come along with us. We were to join the *"Lyngen"* at Tromso. (It was only recently, on rereading an account of the Gladiators in Norway, that I found that this little ship, with its light icebreaker capability, had been used in support of the Gladiator operations in 1940, in which Baldy Donaldson was involved). There was also a sister ship, which I saw in Harstad in late 1959 or early 1960, the *"Managen"*. We flew up to Bardufoss and thence by bus to Tromso. I had fond memories of the calm sea over which we had flown in 1943 and was looking forward to sitting on deck observing the whales. But the weather, as we left Tromso, and came out of the fjord into the open Barents Sea, was something very different: The Barents was to provide a full gale. I was alone in the fo'c'sle cabin while Mother and Valerie were in the First Class cabins aft. Other cabins near the fo'c'sle were occupied by a Norwegian lady and her children, en route to join her husband at the mines at Ny Aalsund. At about 3am the ship's fire alarm sounded and I found myself carrying children up onto the deck of the heaving *"Lyngen"*, where we were to find it was a false alarm – someone having slipped against the button on the bridge. I do not think Mother and Valerie woke at all. The other passengers included an American couple. While Mother and Valerie had their meals aft, the Norwegian family and I had ours in the forward dining saloon.

We did not stop off at Bear Island for the usual cod fishing interlude, but went on, not seeing another vessel until we entered the calm waters of the Ice Fjord. It had become calmer as we got into the lee of the Island and we did see two small whales, but no more during the whole voyage. We passed a Soviet collier by the entrance to Green Harbour and I noticed how much restoration and addition had taken place between Barentsburg and Grumant. We sailed along to Longyearby, where we came alongside the pier and were able to go ashore. We walked along the track to the old Advental airstrip and visited the Junkers Ju.88 wreckage, now considerably broken up by the yearly spring thaws and torrents which come over the area. There was a Snow Bunting nesting in the fuselage. Now, a proper airstrip has been built a bit further north and this is used by Norwegian Boeing 737s, possibly DC-9s and a regular Tu-154 service by Aeroflot from Murmansk.

That afternoon we sailed around Ice Fjord, seeing the beautiful cliffs of temple Fjord, still with many late nesting seabirds. It was noticeable here that the ice cap had receded. We went along, not too far from the north shore with its glaciers and slowed down for the night, cruising off Prince Charles Foreland towards Ny Aalsund, the most northerly town in the world at the time, where we arrived in the early morning. We went ashore and walked around the town and along the shore towards the King's glacier at the head of King's Bay. On the shore had been the place where Amundsen had kept his aircraft and the airship "Norge" had been moored before the war. The various fjords, such as the Cross Fjord to the north from King's Bay, had been the scene of German weather station activity during the war, the stations being supplied by U-boat and aircraft drops. We sailed that evening and near midnight were passing through Cross and smaller fjords with small icefloes in them. Next morning we were off Danes Island, Virgohamn, where in July 1897, the Swedish balloonist Andree and his two companions set off to fly across the pole by balloon. They disappeared, to be discovered on White Island in August 1930. We went ashore here to find masses of small iron bits and pieces, with which Andree and his men had made their hydrogen. This was about the most northern part of our voyage – the pack ice was not far north and we did not venture towards it. We were about fifteen miles short of 80°N.

From Danes Island we moved south and anchored in Magdalena Bay; going ashore in a small motor boat and then along close to the edge of the glacier and among the numerous small and larger ice floes, with their varying colours of blue and green according to the sort of water from which they were formed. The sea was teeming with planktonic life, creatures of curious shapes and no doubt rich food for the fish and up the chain of arctic life. Various noises were tried to make the glacier calve, but without success. This part of the visit was later spoilt by the wish of the American tourist to shoot at seals, fortunately without success, and with considerable protest from me. My daughter was very upset. As he was already booked to leave the ship at Ny Aalsund to go on a polar bear hunting voyage – for which I wished him no success – it was a stupid violation of this particularly beautiful spot and its proper inhabitants. It would have been quite a different matter if we were depending on seal-meat for food.

While on this expedition, Mother solemnly changed for dinner every evening. She had already surprised a team of English students who were walking near Ny Aalsund. For when they came round a rock on a glacier moraine, they had seen an English lady of seventy-six, albeit in trousers, striding easily over the uneven surface. It gave me great amusement during our rough voyage back to Norway to peep into the first class dining saloon porthole to see Mother, neatly dressed for dinner, at the table with the be-sweatered students around her.

Our voyage back, the last of the year and hence the cause of some celebration by the Norwegians on leaving Longyearby, was nearly as rough as the one up – so much for my memories of glassy seas of 1943. We were soon back in the Oslo flat. It had been well worth the journey to see the great peaks and glaciers again

– the Arctic calls one back even more strongly than other more hospitable landscapes.

We had another pleasant autumn and then another winter, with skiing by daylight and by floodlight, up on the tracks around the top of Holmenkollen. A few more flights in the Piper; a trip up to Harsted in Northern Norway, writing an exercise scenario and then a posting back to RAF Colerne, near Bath as Wing Commander Administration.

I arrived there to find that the Air Officer Commanding's inspection was about a fortnight away. "How is your drill?" asked Peter Fleming, our CO, I replied that when I was last on a parade ground, we had been forming fours.

"Oh God!" was Peter's reply.

However, the day came and, as I reported to the AOC-in-C, Air Marshal Barnett, I noticed a smile on his face and perhaps the faint sign of a wink. All went well. The following year our inspection was by our immediate Air Officer, Air Vice-Marshal Peter Wykeham, a man of great character and a sensitive writer, quite apart from his war record. He was affectionately known as the Barnet(t) By-Pass, because of his independent actions! While at Colerne we also had two Battle of Britain Open Days, which required a great deal of preparation, especially by my colleague, OC (Officer Commanding) Flying Wing, my wing was concerned with a lot of the ground housekeeping.

At this time Colerne had a small collection of historical aircraft and a communications flight on the camp, I decided to do some more flying, perhaps graduating to the Hastings at a later date. But at the same time, I decided to increase my life insurance and here I ran straight into the matter of the heart condition. My own company at once wanted to load the policy and another company, which said it could meet my case, failed to do so when it examined the situation. There was nothing to do but to refer the matter of the contradiction of "fit-full-flying" of the RAF and the views of the insurance companies. The result, after extensive medicals, was a ruling that I was unfit, I could continue on until age fifty-five in the same rank, no prospect of flying again or promotion, or invaliding. I was forty-two, so I decided on the latter course. A later attempt to argue before a tribunal that the infarct was the result of service – and particularly that in Poland – failed, but was an interesting exercise. Shortly before Christmas 1961, we left Colerne. It had been a useful time with interesting work, particularly that involving people and the Station Institute Committee work. There was one very curious ornithological experience, too. Our married quarter roof was invaded by starlings and the Works and Buildings moved in to evict. In fact they walled in a nest of young, but my wife, supported by Peter Fleming, had them brought out and it was hoped that the parents would feed them. No such luck, and 'Vera, aided by Eddie Fleming, brought them up in the spare room, Eddie providing worms from her older garden. Each bird was given a Russian name; Poposhkin, Totoshkin, Momoshkin and Kokoshkin and each was ringed with a coloured ring to distinguish them one from each other. When they were ready, they were released and flew away; no one came back to hand, but Totoshkin stayed around for a day or so. Then he too left. But there is a sequel, two years or so later, I was in a hide at Minsmere, watching rather more exotic birds than starlings, when a starling with a yellow ring walked into the field of view of my binoculars. Who else would have put a ring on a Starling? The distance of 180 or so miles does not mean much, but the appearance of the possible Totoshkin two years later is a bit of a coincidence. We also had bred canaries from the two birds we brought back from Norway, the cock lived to the age of fourteen, but one of the young ones, who got stuck in hatching and was teased out of his eggshell by me with needles, lived until the age of eighteen!

With us into retirement went Tramp, the fine old mongrel, whom we had acquired at Colerne, when his owners had to go to Cyprus. Tramp was a delight to us until his death in early 1970. He was an inveterate motorist and enjoyed singing RAF songs as he drove. His favourite being the old Sullom Voe song "They sent us off to Norway . . . W" to the tune of John Brown's body.

Some people say their dogs enjoy television, but Tramp took no notice of it, until one day there was a Sunday broadcast of hymns from RAF Cranwell and the "Battle Hymn of the Republic" was sung. Tramp at once lifted his head and hit the note for the chorus and seemed mightily surprised that I did not join in. In his early life he had been a farm dog, but strayed onto Colerne camp, where he was chased by service police and was acquired by his owners, the Blicks, when under sentence of death. Before we had him, he had fathered a litter of puppies outside the NAAFI shop when on a shopping expedition with Pam Blick. We were invited to go and see the puppies. The bitch not only proudly showed them to the proud father, but then ran off to play with him, before we returned. When Peter Fleming was on leave and I was acting CO, Tramp would travel with me in the official car with the flag. We would be saluted as we passed the guardroom, but this did not prevent my passenger from growling at the sight of the smartly blancoed belts of the service police. He would come to the office, as would Peter Fleming's dogs, but for Tramp this soon had to cease, for he ran into the CO's office in front of me, raised his leg against the desk in recognition of the situation, vis-à-vis the absent CO's bitch and then jumped full tilt out of the window, making a beeline for the NAAFI shop and chocolate from the girls serving in the shop.

CHAPTER SEVENTEEN

Civil Servant – The World of Customs and Beyond

In early 1962, as part of my retirement leave, we managed to take a skiing holiday, combined with some market research on the way through France, on the Franco-Swiss border at Morgins.

We returned to England and I started doing some more market research assignments for John Costello, who had worked and flown with me at the Air Ministry. This was useful and I also continued with my scanning and translation, mainly from the Soviet press, for the *Aeroplane and Commercial Aviation News* and later for *Flight International* and for *RAF Flying Review*, later to evolve into *Air International* with William Green. This work, I had started at the request of Thurstan James, when still at Colerne. Thurstan James was then the Editor of the *Aeroplane*. There was also the need to prepare for the Civil Service examinations, which I had decided to take. These were taken, but unfortunately the Foreign Office seemed unlikely to be using my services in Eastern Europe, where my interest lay and talked about Africa and South America. These areas would have been wonderful from the point of view of general and particularly natural history interest. However, security took a hand, these were the days of the Barbara Fell case, the criteria changed and my wife was Russian born. So

I was told that I would be offered a job in the Home Civil Service.

Meanwhile, Vera and I had been on our first visit together to the USSR, we went to Moscow and Leningrad. It was a fascinating visit and being longer than the previous one, gave time to enjoy the two cities. We visited many places in Moscow and also went out to the Monastery of Zagorsk. For Vera this was a great experience to return to the land of her birth and she was made very welcome, everyone being interested that she spoke such good Russian after her years as an émigré. During the time in Moscow we met one of her aunts who came up from Rostov-on-Don to see us. There was also the big event of the first double space flight of Vostocks 3 and 4 – Nikolaev and Popovich – we were there for their launch and for their return. The celebrations of the latter brought official and one unofficial march out on the streets of Moscow, while helicopters dropped leaflets on the crowd. In Leningrad, we visited both Peterhof and Pushkin (the former Tsarskoye Tselo) and the Arctic museum, where I was delighted to see the pioneer Polar aviator Babushkin's aircraft preserved. We also enjoyed an extensive visit to the Hermitage, the latter when we visited the great cemetery and memorial to the dead of Leningrad and where relations of Vera were buried. We were to make a further visit (of a week) in 1965, for the *Aeroplane and Commercial Aviation News*, to get material for two articles on Aeroflot. When resting from aircraft, we visited the Zoological Museum and had a chance meeting and talk with one of the world's greatest ornithologists, the late G. P. Dementiev.

In the first article I made a rather striking comparison between the loads carried during the whole of the initial Soviet civil airlines operation between Moscow and Nizhny Novgorod (now Gor'ky) in 1923 and the fact that a single Tu-114 could carry the same load of passengers and mail in one flight. For some years this comparison, later to be updated to the Ilyushin Il-62, was used by the Soviet Minister of Civil Aviation and even higher members of the Soviet Government, up to Mr Brezhnev, in speeches and articles. So I had an achievement in that, even if my own official drafts as a civil servant for Treasury Ministers' letters, or answers in the House, did not meet with the same success, rarely getting unamended past the Assistant Secretary, on at least one occasion I had the pleasure of quoting the names of my more satisfied "clients"!

I had to make a choice of which Civil Service department I would like to join. Rather without hope I put down the Ministry of Defence (Air); for second choice I specified, because of my small medical past, the Ministry of Health; finally, because I was interested in the chemistry and manufacture (and consumption) of wines and spirits, I put Customs and Excise as third choice. Customs it was to be and I was appointed as a Principal.

I arrived in due course at King's Beam House, the London head office of Customs, and I became a member of the International Division. The country was hovering on the brink of the Common Market then, in early 1963, there was to be a big UN Conference on the facilitation of travel and tourism in Rome later in the summer. So, while there was not a lot of immediate and urgent work on hand, there was plenty of time to read oneself in, to get to know the procedures and the specialized language.

The conference at Rome was excellent, not least because I had never been to that city. There was also the opportunity on the flight out to Rome on the BEA Comet, to send a note to the Captain, which resulted in an invitation to the flight deck while we crossed the Alps and began the descent downhill to Rome. Pre-hijacking days, of course! The preparation for the Conference had involved the study of many papers and I think my only real contribution was to suggest that the committee looked again at the draft speech for the ambassador at the opening of the Conference. This read in one part: "Foreign travel gives an enormous opportunity for intercourse between people of different nationalities." This sentence had nearly got through, but I like to think that my intervention in preventing this use of a word with a then rather more modern meaning, had saved a gaffe for the former aviation person, Sir John Ward.

There was friendly contact with the Soviet delegation at the Conference, with whom the committee found many points on which we saw eye-to-eye on customs matters. We also shared some amused surprise when our Afghan colleagues expressed an apparently strongly held wish that all travellers should have the right to carry a TV set, along with all the other paraphernalia of travellers, without a Customs eyebrow being raised. No doubt now Kabul has its own TV service, but at the time it seemed an improbable area to show such a heartfelt wish for such a concession.

The Conference proceedings were frequently interrupted whenever the South African delegate rose to his feet to speak, because then, the other African countries' delegations ostentatiously walked out. We had one hot afternoon when it was noticed that one of our African friends had failed to go out because he was asleep! As we all felt like doing! Sadness fell on the conference when the senior Swiss delegate, returning from a weekend at home, was killed when his aircraft crashed (Caravelle). The members of the Conference were all invited to meet the then new Pope (Paul VI) at Castel Gandolfo, which was a moving experience for all. All the delegates spent much time sightseeing in and round about Rome, both on their own and with the assistance of the Italian Tourist authorities.

After returning to London there were other minor conferences on international transport to attend in Geneva. One memorable morning things were a bit held up, for the French had suddenly closed a Customs frontier post it was said, without warning, which was extensively used by TIR lorry traffic, thoroughly embarrassing the Swiss, who were left with a long line on their side of the frontier. It was a good lesson to remember for later days, on what to avoid. The argument went on for some time.

One of the delights of working in London was the renewal of shopping at lunchtime in Soho and elsewhere at the familiar

shops of a few years back, such as Hamburger Products in
Brewer Street, Berwick Street Market and the fish shops. One day
I was walking past a new Strip Club and I was amused to hear
the girl at the door announcing, in spite of the snow and sleet
which was falling, "All our girls strip quite naked". I remarked
that I hoped they'd not catch cold on such a day and this, needless to say, started some backchat. It was at this club too, that I
saw one of those mysterious and inexplicable events, a powerful
American matron leading her rather trailing husband into the
establishment.

Another reflection of life in the early seventies was when I
was returning from a shopping expedition. As usual I got into the
rear non-smoking Circle Line carriage at Charing Cross
(Embankment). Two young teenage boys were smoking in it, but,
before I could remonstrate, two men in their twenties with shopping bags, roundly told the boys to stop smoking and, if they
wanted to do so, to get into another carriage at Temple Station.
The boys did this, but as we pulled out of Temple, the two men
got syringes from their bags and each took an injection of some
drug!

There were also the various observations of birds in the centre
of London, particularly of Kestrels. One pair attempted to nest on
the new Commercial Union building, and once, five were flying
around it (outside the breeding season), one was also seen by me
in the Chancery Lane area above the traffic. But the best observation was when a Kestrel flew past the window of a King's Beam
House office while a rather dull meeting was in progress. I was
fascinated to see that it had a mouse in its beak.

A very odd situation arose when I was walking one day, bowler
hatted with brief case in hand, down Eastcheap, near to one of the
side turnings, where in various shops, eels are cut up for jellied
eels. In the rainwater in the street gutter, an eel, no doubt escaped
from a box, was swimming. I picked it up and set off before I was
stopped, down towards the Monument, across to a point where
I knew there was good access to the river above London Bridge.

There, I flung the eel as far as I could, out into the river. It swam for a minute on the surface and then disappeared. There was a cough behind me. I looked around and there was a man who said, "If I hadn't seen that, I'd never have believed it. I saw you pick up the eel and had to follow you down here to see what you'd do with it."

After about eighteen months in the International Division, I was moved to Purchase Tax Liability.

During these years in London, several things happened. Firstly in 1962, just before I joined the department, I read in the *Times* of the publication in the journal *"Novy Mir"* of the story, *"One day in the life of Ivan Denisovic"*, by one Alexander Solzhenitsyn. I quickly got hold of a copy, read the story and became a subscriber to *"Novy Mir"*. I was fascinated by this story, not so much by its content, but the fact that it had been published at all. What a change this was since the days of 1945 – 1952 and up to the death of Stalin! The decision to publish such stories was potentially dangerous, in the mistaken eye of many of the authorities, to the Soviet scheme of things.

In 1966, I read a story in *"Novy Mir"* entitled *"Farewell Gul'sary!"* by the Kirgiz author, Chingiz Aitmatov. This is the story of a horse and his master. It made a profound impression on both my wife and myself. For me it gave me an insight into the author's mind and I realized that here was a man with whom I could at once find rapport, friendship and understanding. For over two years I thought about this story and its author, reading it over and over again. Finally one day my wife asked, "Why don't you translate it?" I decided I must and wrote to Chingiz Aitmatov for his consent. A letter quickly came back with his agreement and then began a correspondence which I value greatly. Hodder and Stoughton published the story in 1970. Chingiz came over for the launching, bringing with him his son, Sanzhar, and they came to stay with us at home in Felixstowe.

In 1972 my wife and I went again to the USSR, visiting Frunze (via Moscow). We spent about a week in the Kirgiz Republic, met Chingiz and his family and saw Kirgizia for ourselves. We went on to Tashkent, Samarkend, Sochi and then back to Moscow where we spent some happy hours with Georgi Vladimov, his wife and mother-in-law.

Kirgizia made a very deep impression on us. Having lived with the story of "Gul'sary", I had already formed a mental picture of the country and its scenery and people, but reality was even better. Unfortunately, there was far too little one could see in just a week. We only saw the foothills of the Tyan-Shan, we were unable, through pressure of time, to reach Issyk Kul', the great lake, but what we saw was enough to wish to go back and see more. We had a happy day at the nature reserve at Tokmak, some miles to the east of Frunze where, at a small meeting in our honour, I suddenly found myself addressing the company in Russian after a fine meal. During this, as chief guest, I was given the honour of carving and serving the head of the lamb. No easy task after so many years away from anatomy, let alone the lavish hospitality which had included kumys as well as more powerful beverages. One of the company has since died, as Chingiz wrote and told us not so long ago, it is a measure of the power of the country and its people that we could feel personal grief too, after such short acquaintance with him.

Thus have developed two of the friendships, long wished for, and a wish dating from my days in Poland, but what fine friends I have found!

Incidentally, it was fascinating to walk through the streets of Frunze, those cool and shady streets, and to hear coming from an open window the sounds of a radio, a western broadcast;

"I beg your pardon; I never promised you a rose garden . . ." For all the steps forward and some backward, things had changed a very great deal since the stern days of Stalin which I had experienced in Poland twenty-three years and less before.

*　　*　　*

At the end of 1970 I had left the head office of Customs and Excise in London and had taken up a post as an Assistant Collector in Harwich (now East Anglia) Collection, with the main responsibility for Felixstowe. For nearly seven years, nearly four of them on my own, I was in the centre of the Customs side of the growth of this remarkable port and working closely with the successive management figures of the Felixstowe Dock and Railway Company, as well as with excellent colleagues of all grades. Moreover, I was able to keep up some of the firm friendships I had made in London.

The founding of the RAF Ornithological Society in 1965, when I was asked to become treasurer, and an increase in my bird observations, including photography, particularly with Herbert and Joan Axell, had been a busy feature of my spare time. It was a little comical though, when reading after work, I was taking photographs of a Spoonbill near the Felixstowe Dock with my big telephoto lens, suddenly the law arrived in the form of two policemen in a car, summoned by some public-spirited citizen who thought, I suppose, a spy was at work. No offence was, of course, being committed, one of the policemen, on being told by me what I was doing could not contain himself, he too was an ornithologist, "What, a Spoonbill? Please let me have a look at it!"

But to return to work. During the period from 1970 there were many changes to be weathered in Customs. There was the re-organization of the Department and my move out to Harwich collection had been a small part of that.

In the spring of 1978 I found, as I had found for a time in 1974, that increasing pressures of work (the changes of the last four years with the introduction of EEC procedures, the great growth of numbers of staff in post and the growth of the port of Felixstowe as a whole; entirely new factors resulting from the impending introduction of data processing and the Preventative Review), were all beginning to give me much worry and to tell on my efficiency and health. So I was retired, at my own request, on health grounds in June 1978.

But, like Ulysses, I feel that "still some work of noble note may yet be done", if only in matters which interest me, but I hope especially so in the field of translation and in the introduction of more Soviet literature to the English reader.

I hope these pages show in telling this story, incomplete as it may be, and in remembering some of those who, too, wished to live, that:-

"No one is forgotten, nothing is forgotten."

(Leningrad Piskarevskoye Memorial).

Index